LONGER HOURS, FEWER JOBS

Employment and Unemployment in the United States

MICHAEL D. YATES

MONTHLY REVIEW PRESS
NEW YORK

Library of Congress Cataloging-in-Publication Data
Yates, Michael, 1946-
    Longer hours, fewer jobs : employment and unemployment in the United States /
by Michael Yates.
        p. cm. — (Cornerstone books)
    Includes bibliographical references.
    ISBN 0-85345-888-X
    1. Unemployment—United States. 2. Labor market—United States. 3. Over-
time—United States. 4. Hours of labor—United States. 5. Wages—United
States. 6. Cost and standard of living—United States. 7. Income distribution—
United States. 8. Quality of life—United States. I. Title. II. Series: Cornerstone
books (New York, N.Y.)
HD5724.Y38 1993
331.1'0973—dc20   93-26615
                                                       CIP

Monthly Review Press
122 West 27th Street
New York, NY 10001

Manufactured in the United States of America
10 9 8 7 6 5 4 3 2 1

To my grandmother Lucille,
whose strength in the face of a hard life
has helped me to see things clearly

CONTENTS

ACKNOWLEDGMENTS

I want to thank Susan Lowes and the staff at Monthly Review Press for their unfailingly kind, courteous, and professional assistance. I also want to thank John Bellamy Foster for reading the manuscript and making several helpful suggestions, as well as Teresa Amott for permission to use several of the figures from her fine book, *Caught in the Crisis: Women and the U.S. Economy Today* (also in the Cornerstone series). Finally, I want to thank Karen Korenoski and our children, Tara, Thian, Rethe, and Zane, for their support and encouragement. Without them, the madness that is this country would be almost too much to bear.

1

INTRODUCTION:
THE AMERICAN CENTURY

My father got out of the Navy in 1945 after three years in the South Pacific, just in time to join a picket line at the Pittsburgh Plate Glass Company's largest plant in Ford City, Pennsylvania. Like millions of workers around the country, he and his workmates struck to reverse the deterioration of their purchasing power and working conditions brought about by wartime controls on labor. When the strike ended, he settled into thirty-eight years of packing, cutting, and inspecting plates of glass. Business was good and in all of that time he was never laid off. It was the "American Century": we had won the great war and now we were reaping the spoils. The rest of the world needed American goods, and the government gave them money to buy those goods—provided they rebuilt their economies along lines pleasing to us and provided they did not object to our businesses operating in their countries. Here at home, people had all the money that they had not been able to spend during the war. The government kept its spending high, building weapons and roads and lending the returning soldiers money to buy houses and go to college. My dad and his buddies won that strike, and so did their brothers and sisters in steel, coal, rubber, auto, and electronics. Wages began to rise; so did fringe benefits.

All the cars and houses that people bought kept the plates of glass rolling off the assembly line. Men brought home paychecks fat with incentive pay and overtime. This money, spent and re-spent, kept the town's stores, gas stations, and movie houses hopping. The town grew and families prospered. I was born in 1946, the first year of the baby boom, so I grew up during the postwar expansion. I was optimistic about my future. I do not remember ever worrying about finding a job. I was good in school and got a college scholarship, but if I had not been, I could have gone to work with my father, or in another mill. In college, I studied what interested me. I believed that no matter what I learned, I would get a good job when I graduated. I liked college so much that I just stayed there, figuring that I would be a teacher. And that is what I did. The war in Vietnam almost messed up my plans, and, looking back, I see that horrible and immoral war as the event that marked the end of the American Century. But at the time I was simply considered lucky. I avoided the draft and did what I wanted. I got in under the gun, so to speak, grabbing the last piece of a pie that we expected to keep on growing.

The American Century is dead and gone. In its place we have a society coming apart at the seams. The national unemployment rate has not been below 5 percent since 1973, which means that at no time during the Reagan "boom" of the 1980s were there fewer than 6 million unemployed by the government's own count. The purchasing power of our weekly earnings is no higher now than it was in 1967. We have been able to maintain our standards of living only by working more hours or sending more family members into the workforce. Yet in the last few years family income has also begun to fall. Our children have not faced a bleaker future since the Great Depression of the 1930s. There are not enough jobs to go around, and even fewer good jobs. As businesses have mastered the art of producing anywhere in the world, plants are being closed—not only when they cannot make profits but when the profits they make are not high enough.

Along with falling wages and bloated unemployment lines, there has been a shocking increase in inequality and poverty. The working class has been looted, its income given to the rich, who are wealthier now than at any time since World War II. Between 1963 and 1983, the richest 1/2 percent of all families saw their wealth rise by 9.7 percent, while the poorest 90 percent suffered a 6.7 percent loss.[1] Average real family income fell for the poorest 60 percent of all families between 1977 and 1990, but it increased by 33.2 percent for the richest 20 percent and by a staggering 95.1 percent for the richest 1 percent.[2] The government's poverty level is barely enough to live on, yet there are more than 30 million people living below it. It is estimated that by the year 2000 one of every three children will be poor.[3] Needless to say, poverty is disproportionately the lot of women and people of color. More than one-third of all black people and people in female-headed households are poor.[4]

Low income and high unemployment have bred the profound social breakdown we see every night on the television news. Homelessness, disease, mental illness, murder, and physical violence are epidemic. I was in Canada recently and was amazed at how much attention the media gave to one abduction and rape. If our media did this for every rape in the United States, there would be no room for anything else.

Well, a cynic might say, you have painted an ugly picture, but things were not all that wonderful during your American Century. Black citizens did not have it so good: in your own hometown, they had to live in crummy houses at the "lower end." And the unions began to decline in the middle of the 1950s. Throughout the postwar boom, employers developed labor-saving and skill-reducing technology that eroded union power. When my father's local struck in 1958 rather than agree to a radical reorganization of the workplace, the company began to move the work to nonunion plants. From then on, employment fell.

No doubt the United States between 1946 and 1970 had its share of misery. However, a sizable fraction of the working class experienced previously undreamed-of improvements in their standard of living. Things are different now, and people want to know why. In this book, I will try to answer this question. What we will find is that the American Century inevitably created the seeds of its own destruction, as has every boom under our economic system. When we put the postwar boom into historical perspective, we will see that it was but one among many, and that today's depression is also only one among many. Our system cannot grow without contracting, and employment cannot exist without unemployment. We will learn that while the current period is unique in many ways, in other respects it is not. We will learn that, under our economic system, many things can be done to make life better, and we will learn how we might make these things happen. But we will also learn that the cycles of boom and bust and the poles of wealth and poverty cannot be eliminated unless and until we are willing to contemplate an entirely new organization of our production and distribution.

In addition to this introduction, there are five chapters. Chapters 2 and 3 examine the problem of *employment.* They show that less and less employment is "good" employment. Most jobs do not pay enough to support a family, while many do not even pay enough to put a family above the government's poverty level. Part-time and temporary employment abound, and benefits are decreasing or are inaccessible. Very few new entrants into the labor force can count on finding a high-paying, secure job like the ones my father and I had. To keep up their living standards, many workers have been forced to increase their hours of work by working overtime, moonlighting, or both. For the first time since the middle of the nineteenth century, we are working more for less money.

The problem of *employment* is closely connected to the problem of *unemployment,* the subject of Chapter 4. The normal operation of our economic system makes it impossible for everyone who wants a job to find one. That is, unemployment is created as employers go about their normal business. As we shall see, the crisis in which our economy has been mired for the past two decades has greatly swelled the ranks of the unemployed. This burgeoning army of job seekers generates a host of problems in its own right, but it also wreaks havoc on the employed by intensifying the competition for jobs. Paradoxically, the result is that while the hours many people work are increasing, a growing number cannot find any work at all.

Chapter 5 examines the twin problems of employment and unemployment by demonstrating that they are the result of the ceaseless drive by our business enterprises to make money—or, as we shall put it, to accumulate capital. Our theory will be a radical one by comparison to the explanations offered by more "respectable" opinion. But, as we shall see, no other comes close to adequately explaining the dismal state of the working classes.

Chapter 6 provides some suggestions for creating an economy in which people can do meaningful work and live decently. Since our analysis will lead us to the conclusion that it is in the interest of those who now wield economic and political power that most people be denied this opportunity, we shall have to organize ourselves to force the issue. There are possibilities for both the employed and the unemployed to organize, although I believe that the best chance for building effective organizations rests with the employed. A precondition for any progressive program is thus the building of a multiethnic, multinational, and nonsexist working-class movement, both at the level of the workplace and at the level of society. As we begin to build such a movement, we can also demand the full employment, universal health care, labor law reform, and controls on capital that will strengthen the movement and make a better life for workers here and throughout the world.

2

EMPLOYMENT: FALLING WAGES AND INCOMES

SOME OMINOUS TRENDS

The working class is comprised of those who are employed and those who are unemployed. In this and the next chapter, we look at the employed. What can we say about those who are working? What has been happening to their wage rates and incomes, their hours of work, the quality of their jobs? A quick look at the trends is not encouraging.

The income that a working person makes depends on his or her hourly wage rate and the number of hours worked. The actual wage rate (what economists call the *nominal* wage rate) is not the important number, because even if it rises, a worker may be worse off if prices rise faster. Therefore the nominal wage rate must be adjusted for inflation. This gives us the *real* wage rate—the purchasing-power wage rate. By comparing real wage rates in different time periods, we can tell if the purchasing power of the nominal wage rate has increased or decreased.

Overall, real wage rates rose throughout the long boom from 1945 to 1970. This trend was then reversed: real hourly wage rates are no higher at present than they were in 1973. This means that the average nominal hourly wage rate of all workers in this country will buy no more goods and services now than it would have bought twenty years ago. If we look at the census category "production and non-supervisory" workers, who make up 80 percent of the workforce and are the people we generally mean when we use the term "working class," the trend is worse. The working class's real hourly wage rate was *lower* in 1991 than it was in 1973. In fact, between 1979 and 1989, the average real hourly wage rate of the working class fell by 0.7 percent *per year*. Average real weekly earnings fell by 1.0 percent per year over the same period. Adding fringes, such as health and pension benefits, to real hourly wage rates moderates these declines, but total compensation for all workers still fell by 8.6 percent between 1977 and 1992.[1]

CALCULATING REAL WAGES Suppose that the economy produced only one good. Your wage rate is $5.00 per hour, and the price of the good is $1.00. Then the purchasing power of your nominal wage of $5.00 is 5 units of the good, which we get by dividing the nominal wage rate by the price of the good. If the price rose to $2.00, the purchasing power or real wage rate is 2.5, or $5.00 divided by $2.00. Of course, in the real world there are millions of goods, so we cannot just divide by a price. Instead, we must calculate an average price. This is done by constructing a price index, the most common of which is the Consumer Price Index, or CPI. The CPI measures the change in the price of a "market basket" of commonly consumed goods and services. The items in the basket are weighted according to their importance in peoples' budgets. One year is chosen as the "base year," and the price of the basket in any year is compared to the price in the base year. If the basket costs more in one year than in the base year, it must be because prices have risen, since the quantity of goods in the basket is the same every year. The price of the basket is set equal to 100 in the base year and is higher or lower in any given year depending upon whether prices have risen or fallen. A CPI of 120 means that the price of the basket is 20 percent higher than in the base year; a CPI of 91 means that the cost of the goods in the basket is 9 percent lower than in the base year. To calculate the real wage rate, we simply take the nominal wage rate and divide it by the CPI. If we want the real wage to have the same number of digits as the nominal wage, we can multiply the result by 100. For example, suppose your hourly wage rate was $9.00 in 1980 and $11.00 in 1992. The CPI in 1980 was 82.4, and in 1990 it was 130.7 (the base year is the average of the price of the market basket between 1982 and 1984). Dividing $9.00 by 82.4 and $11.00 by 130.7 gives us real hourly wage rates of $10.92 and $8.42. Therefore, your real hourly wage rate fell by 23 percent in ten years, that is, each dollar you earned in 1990 bought only 77 percent of what it would have bought in 1980.

Major changes have also taken place in the number of hours worked. To compensate for the decline in real wage rates, people have had to work longer hours. Beginning in the late 1960s, the United States entered what economist Juliet Schor calls "an era of rising worktime." Schor estimates that the average employed person worked 163 more hours per year in 1987 than in 1969, an amount equal to an extra month of work.[2] This trend continued until 1990, when hours fell slightly because of the recession.[3] Hours of work per year rose much more for women than for men—305 hours for women and 98 for men.[4] Over the same 1969 to 1987 period, men increased their household work by 68 hours and women *decreased* theirs by 145 hours (though women still do most household work), so that total hours of work, market plus household, rose considerably for both men and women.[5] Needless to say, there is a connection between shrinking real wages and rising hours of work: the only way that working-class families have been able to keep up or increase their standard of living has been to increase their hours of labor. More family members have entered the labor force, and family members have worked more hours. All of this has placed tremendous stress on families, with results that are the daily fare of the tabloids and talk shows.

Finally, the nature of the work people do has undergone profound change. We are all aware that hundreds of thousands of manufacturing jobs have disappeared, making it practically impossible for those with a high school diploma or less to get decent-paying employment. Now these people can aspire to work in the service sector—in fast-food restaurants, in offices, and in hospitals, selling junk food and mopping floors. In addition, there has been an enormous growth of "contingent" work, which can be defined as "jobs that do not fit the traditional description of a full-time, permanent job with benefits."[6] Contingent work includes part-time work, temporary work, and contract work. Involuntary part-time work has grown 121 percent between 1970 and 1990. Temporary employment, including workers leased by employee-leasing companies, grew 300 percent between 1982 and 1990, until it totalled 1.295 million people in 1990.[7] Contract workers are those who work for a contractor rather than a permanent employer or contract out their own services. Employers are now moving workers from the status of employee to that of independent contractor to avoid paying both legally required and employer-provided benefits. No hard data exist on the number of contract workers, although the number of people "reporting income only as self-employed or independent contractors grew 53.6 percent, from 6.2 to 9.5 million, between 1985 and 1988."[8] All told, there are between 29.9 and 36.6 million contingent workers, or between 25 and 30 percent of the labor force.[9]

One last aspect of the changing nature of the job market that deserves our attention is the level of skill necessary for most work. We are bombarded with propaganda about how the jobs of the future will require high skill levels, so we had better get more education to prepare us to do them. However, it is not at all obvious that this is the case. Skill requirements can increase in any of three ways. First, there may be a shift toward *occupations* that require higher levels of skill. Second, there may be a shift toward *industries* that require higher levels of skill. Third, *specific jobs* may have greater skill requirements. There is some evidence of the first shift, but it is expected to slow down markedly over the next decade. For example, a shift toward executive, professional, and managerial jobs—those ordinarily associated with higher skills—is predicted to increase hourly compensation (a proxy for skill) by less than 0.5 percent between now and the year 2000.[10] On the other hand, industrial shifts are expected to *lower* hourly compensation, since the shift is toward the service sector, with its lower paying jobs. In terms of actual skill requirements, as opposed to pay levels, the occupational and industrial shifts will certainly not require any massive upgrading. For example, verbal aptitude requirements are expected to grow by less than 0.7 percent between now and the year 2000.[11] It is difficult to find evidence about the skill content of specific jobs but, as we shall see, there are powerful reasons to believe that skill upgrading will always be threatened because it is cheaper to use less skilled labor. Here, we can simply quote from a 1990 survey by the Commission on the Skills of the American Workforce: "Only 5 percent of American employers believe educational and skill requirements are rising significantly, while 80 percent say their primary concern is finding employees with a good work ethic and appropriate social behavior."[12]

Trends in employment, then, are not hopeful. People are working more hours for less money and there is every indication that they will continue to do so. Some workers will be performing more highly skilled work, but not enough to compensate for the millions who will be toiling away at dead-end, unskilled jobs. In the rest of this chapter, we will study the trends in wages and income. In Chapter 3, we will look at hours of work and jobs.

THE MINIMUM WAGE

There is a great variation in wages in our economy. For instance, not all workers suffered a decline in real wages and compensation over the past dozen years: the most severe decline took place among those earning the lowest wages. A good place to begin an examination of wages is therefore with the federal minimum wage, which was established in 1938 by the Fair Labor Standards Act. In 1981, the minimum wage was $3.35 an hour, and it remained there until 1990, when it was raised to $3.80. In 1991, it was raised to its present level of $4.25. But while the minimum wage has risen in nominal terms (remember, the nominal is the actual wage, i.e., $4.25 per hour today and $3.35 in 1981), it has decreased drastically in real terms. This can be seen in Figure 2-1. Between 1967 and 1992, the real value of the minimum wage fell by 20 percent.[13] This means that a person working full-time at the minimum wage in 1992 could buy only 80 percent of what he or she could have bought in 1967.

Another way to look at the decline in the real minimum wage is to compare it with another income yardstick. A good one is the poverty level of income. The federal government calculates this in order to determine how many people are living in poverty. In 1988, for example, the poverty level of income for a family of two was $7,958; for a family of four, it was $12,029. In 1979, a worker who worked full time at the minimum wage could support a

Figure 2-1
Nominal and Real Minimum Wage, 1967–1992

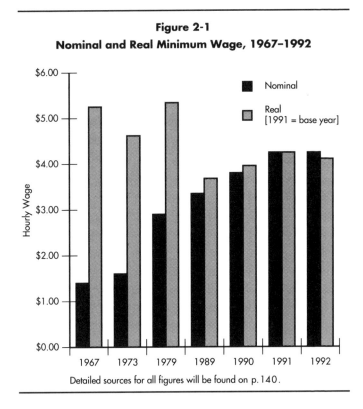

Detailed sources for all figures will be found on p. 140.

family of three at about the poverty level of income. By 1992, this same person's family would be $2,300 *below* the poverty level (in 1991 dollars).[14] Naturally, the situation worsens as the size of the family increases. To stay above the poverty level, the family must either send more members into the workforce and/or increase the hours worked.

It is often argued that the minimum wage applies mainly to teenagers, and it is therefore not that important that it has decreased in real terms. In fact, however, teenagers comprise a relatively small proportion of the minimum-wage workforce. A majority of these workers are women and a sizable number work full time. A person working 40 hours a week for 52 weeks at the current minimum wage would earn the munificent sum of $8,840, far below the poverty level of income for a family of three. The fact that so many women are minimum-wage workers, combined with the rise in the number of households headed by single mothers, goes a long way toward explaining the "feminization of poverty" that we hear so much about in the news. In 1991, 13.9 percent of all persons lived in female-headed households, compared to 8 percent in 1959; the incidence of poverty in such households was 39.7 percent.

Congress has been unwilling to increase the minimum wage enough so that it can support even a small family above poverty. One argument has been that any increase in wage rates would, other things being equal, cause some loss of employment, but in the case of minimum-wage workers this would not be very great. Take, for example, workers employed at McDonald's. Through rigorous time-and-motion studies and the use of technology, McDonald's has made the labor content of its food as low as is currently possible. It could not, therefore, reduce employment if wages increased while still selling the same amount of food. It could raise prices slightly, but this increase would be spread to all consumers, most of whom are not poor. At the same time, those minimum-wage workers who keep their jobs (the vast majority) will have more money to spend and this will increase both the demand for goods and services and employment. It is no wonder that recent studies indicate that raising the minimum wage would be a very good way to reduce poverty.[15] In addition, those workers earning wages just above the current minimum wage would benefit by any increase, since their wages would probably go up in some proportion to the increase in the minimum wage.

THE POVERTY LEVEL OF INCOME The U.S. government first began to estimate a "poverty level" of income in the middle of the 1960s as part of the War On Poverty.[16] The basis for this measure is what is called the "economy food plan," a minimum food budget calculated by the Department of Agriculture that converts the minimum nutritional requirements for a family of four into money. Some very rigid assumptions are built into this conversion. First, it is assumed that the nutritional value of the foods chosen will keep family members in good health over the long run, although other studies have shown that this is not the case. Second, it is assumed that the family will be able to purchase these foods as cheaply as possible—which, given the scarcity of supermarkets in poor neighborhoods and the obvious inability of most people in poverty to buy and store food in bulk, is another unwarranted assumption. Third, it is assumed that the poor can take this cheap food and make maximally nutritious meals from it.

Once the food budget is calculated, it is then assumed that families spend one-third of their total budget on food. This assumption is based on studies done in the 1950s that showed that the average family did indeed allocate its budget in this manner. The poverty level of income for a four-person family is then calculated by multiplying the poverty food budget by three. If, for example, the food budget is $3,000, the poverty level of income is $9,000. The trouble with this procedure is that it is no longer the case that families spend one-third of their incomes on food: today it is much more likely to be between one-fifth and one-sixth. Therefore, using the original procedure, the poverty income should equal the food budget times five or six. Doing the calculation this way would obviously greatly increase the recognized in-

**cidence of poverty. In fact, in 1988 this recalculation
would have increased the poverty rate from 13 percent
to 25.8 percent![17]**

**There are many other problems with the official defini-
tion of poverty, and we will look at them as we go
along. For now, we can simply note that the current procedure allows for no increase in the standard of living of
the officially poor. Most of us would probably say that
what we considered a good life in 1950 involved less
real spending than it would today, but the government
allows for no improvement in what it defines as poverty.**

POVERTY WAGES

If the minimum wage cannot keep a family out of poverty, how
high would wages have to be to do so? What percentage of the
workforce earns less than this? Has this share been rising?

The poverty level of income for a family of four in 1991 was
approximately $13,560. If we consider 2,080 hours per year as
full-time work (40 hours times 52 weeks), it would be necessary to
earn $6.52 an hour to earn this amount, which is $2.27 greater than
the current minimum wage. From 1979 to 1991, there was an
enormous increase in the percentage of all employed people earning
an hourly wage rate that would have placed their yearly income
below the poverty level if they had worked full-time. Low-wage work
has expanded across the board. For example, the fraction of all
workers earning wages the equivalent of only 75 percent of the
poverty level of income tripled between 1979 and 1991, from 4.1
percent to 12.7 percent. The comparable figures for black women
workers are 5.2 percent in 1979 and 19.3 percent in 1991.[18]

The downward shift in wages was matched by a decrease in
the benefits paid poor workers. For instance, if we divide wages
into fifths, we find a 30 percent decline in pension coverage for workers in the poorest fifth between 1979 and 1989,

and a 21 percent decline for those in the next lowest fifth. During the same period, the decline in health coverage for those in the poorest fifth was slightly more than 30 percent.[19] Of course, these same workers were the ones least likely to have such benefits in the first place.

ALTERNATIVE POVERTY MEASURES   The above data show clearly that a significant proportion of the employed earn below poverty level wages and that the wages of the poor have steadily declined. However, it should be remembered that these numbers are based on the official definition of poverty. If the measure were adjusted to take into account the true fraction of poor peoples' incomes spent on food and shelter, the poverty level would be much higher and the number of people in poverty much higher as well. For instance, if increases in the real costs of housing and food are factored in, the poverty rate rises dramatically. Here are the calculations for 1988:

Official poverty measure	13.0 percent
Housing	23.0 percent
Food consumption	25.8 percent[20]

In 1990, such adjustments would raise the poverty level of income for a family of four to over $20,000. At 2,080 hours of work per year, this would require an hourly wage rate of $9.62. A quick look at the help-wanted ads in any newspaper will tell you that not too many jobs pay this much.[21]

ENTRY-LEVEL WAGES

Whether a working person does well or not over the long term depends on the wage rate at which he or she begins work. For example, at my own place of employment, I began work in 1969

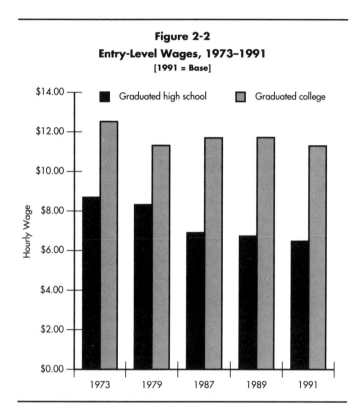

Figure 2-2
Entry-Level Wages, 1973–1991
[1991 = Base]

at a very low salary. It took me more than a dozen years to catch up with co-workers who had started at higher wages. Employers who offer long-term employment (of which there are fewer and fewer) typically have lines of employment progression. The salary a worker earns at any step up the line depends on the starting salary. A few workers may jump a few steps, but they are always a small minority.

As the above discussion of minimum and poverty wages might lead us to expect and as Figure 2-2 shows, entry-level wage rates have decreased dramatically over the past twenty years. For high school graduates, entry-level wage rates dropped by 25.4 percent between 1973 and 1991, while those for college graduates fell by 9.8 percent. What makes these figures even more disheartening is that lower wages have not led to more employment. As we shall see, unemployment is on the rise despite the decline in real wages.

THE SUMMER EMPLOYEE AND THE LAWYER   Perhaps a personal anecdote will illustrate the erosion of starting wages. In 1967 I was hired as a summer employee at the Pittsburgh Plate Glass Company plant in my home-town. My pay was $550 per month, or an hourly rate of $3.44. The Consumer Price Index in 1967 was 33.4 (1982/1984=base year), and in 1992 it was 140.3. This means that the 1992 equivalent of my $3.44 per hour wage is $14.45. On the basis of 2,080 hours per year, this comes to a yearly income of $30,056. Just recently, my niece graduated from Duquesne Law School, which is also in Pittsburgh. After an extended job search, she managed to get hired as a clerk for a local judge. Her salary is $28,000 per year, less in hourly terms than what I was paid for doing very little as a summer worker at my father's factory twenty-six long years ago. And you can bet that my niece will be expected to put in more than full-time hours for her pay!

WAGES IN GENERAL

With the exception of those at the very top of the wage pyramid, workers lost ground in terms of wages during the Reagan/Bush years and for nearly a decade before. Workers at nearly all levels of education and experience suffered real wage declines between 1973 and 1991. If we divide workers into five wage groups (called quintiles), those at every quintile break point

(20, 40, 60, 80) experienced a decline in real hourly wage rates between 1973 and 1991.[22] Women in the top quintile were the only group that enjoyed an increased real wage rate. Similarly, all workers lost real fringe benefits. During the earlier part of the 1980s, the poorest, least experienced, and least educated suffered the largest real wage declines. But in the late 1980s and early 1990s, losses moved upward to affect those with higher wages, college degrees, and experience.

Young workers, those with limited work experience, those with less education (i.e., a high school degree or less) have suffered the most. Thus those who are both young and relatively uneducated, especially men, have seen their real hourly wage rates drop precipitously.

GROWING INEQUALITY

While those at the bottom of the wage scale lost large amounts of purchasing power, those in the middle did not lose as much, and those at the very top gained. At the same time, those who get money from their ownership of assets (such as stocks, bonds, and property) flourished during the 1980s. The result of these changes was a more unequal distribution of income—more unequal than at any time since the 1920s.

Income inequality is usually measured in terms of family income. The incomes of all families are ranked, from the lowest to the highest. Then the family incomes are divided into quintiles so that there is the same number of families in each quintile. Next, the total income of each quintile is divided by the total income of all of the quintiles combined, which (multiplied by 100) gives us each quintile's percentage of total family income.

Figure 2-3 shows the strikingly unequal distribution of family incomes in the United States. In fact, it is are more unequal than in any other industrialized nation. What is noteworthy, however, is that the distribution has become markedly *more* unequal over the past twenty years. The poorest two-fifths of families lost

Figure 2-3

Average Income for Family Income Groups, 1992

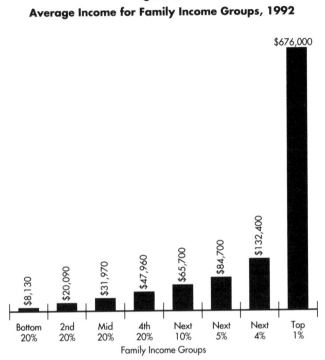

nearly 13 percent of their share of total family income during this period, while the richest fifth *gained* nearly 8 percent. The losses at the bottom can be largely attributed to the falling real wage rates we have documented, along with the savage cuts in government transfer payments to the poor. At the top of the distribution, richer families gained both because their real wages increased and because their incomes from stocks, bonds, and property exploded.[23]

The overall growth in wage and income inequality has been paralleled by inequalities between people of color (blacks and

Hispanics) and whites, and between young and old. The gap between men and women has decreased, but mainly because of the great drop in the real wages of men. Thus between 1979 and 1989, the ratio of female to male median hourly wage rates rose from 62.8 percent to 73.9 percent, but nearly 75 percent of this rise was due to the decline in the median wage rate of men.[24] We have already seen that young workers, blacks, and Hispanics suffered greater wage losses than older white workers, so that the gaps between white and nonwhite and between older and younger workers widened. Finally, the wage differential between those with more and less education has widened since the real wages of the less-educated fell by more than those with college degrees.

Anyway we look at it, the past twelve years, and probably the past two decades, have witnessed rapidly falling real wages and benefits for wide sectors of the working population. Those who began at the bottom have suffered the most, but older, college-educated, and white workers are now under the gun of wage cuts as well. The distributions of income and wealth have become grotesquely unequal.

CONCLUSION

Many people have an image of the United States as a nation dominated by the "middle class," a large and growing group of upwardly mobile workers, professionals, and owners of small businesses. At any given time, some people were poor, but everyone had a chance at the "American Dream" of solid financial success. While this view was always more myth than reality, it can no longer survive even as myth. As the data in this chapter have shown, we appear to be moving toward a two-tier society, with a minority at the top with lots of money and power and the vast majority below and sinking fast, with neither money nor power and precious little hope for the future.

3

EMPLOYMENT: INCREASING HOURS AND JUNK JOBS

FAMILY INCOMES

Between the mid-1970s and the end of the 1980s, family incomes grew despite falling real wage rates (although the rate of growth slowed considerably from that of the post-World War II prosperity and by the beginning of the 1990s had become negative). The trends in median family income growth (in average percent change each year) are shown in Figure 3-1. To put the percentages into perspective, note that, in 1991 dollars, median family income in 1947 was $17,059 and in 1991 was $35,939.

Naturally, the numbers hide a good deal of variability in family income growth because they lump together all ages, races, sexes, and so forth. While some growth was experienced by all types of

Figure 3-1
Changes in Median Family Income, 1947–1991

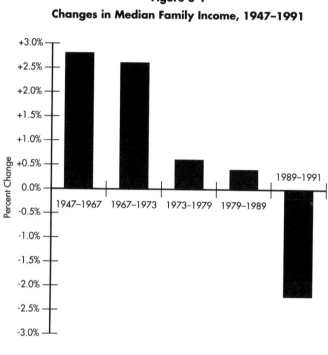

families over this long period, rates of growth were lower for young families, black and Hispanic families, and those headed by women. Young families—those where the household head was under 25—had negative income growth throughout the 1980s (-2.5 percent per year!), as did households headed by a single parent, male or female. Families in the lowest fifth of the income distribution have not seen any income growth since 1973.[1] Interestingly, the elderly fared well in terms of income growth throughout the 1980s thanks to social security. And keep in mind that as family income growth slowed, it also became markedly more unequally distributed.

WOMEN TO THE RESCUE

Suppose we consider a working-class family in the mid-1970s. The husband is working in the labor market and the wife is working at home. The husband's real wage has been rising steadily and the family has made some long-term financial commitments: a home, a car, and a savings fund for the kids' college. Then the husband's real wage rate begins its downward spiral. How will the family fulfill its financial obligations and improve its standard of living? The only way is for it to increase its hours of labor market work. One obvious possibility is for the wife to get a labor market job; another is for the children to go to work.

Consider the following extracts from Juliet Schor's *The Overworked American*:

> Not only are more of the nation's young people working, but they are working longer hours. A 1989 nationwide sweep by government inspectors uncovered wide-scale abuses of child labor laws—violations of allowable hours, permissible activities, and ages of employment.... A New Hampshire study found that 85 percent of the state's tenth- to twelfth-graders hold jobs, and 45 percent of them work more than twenty hours a week.... Teachers report that students are falling asleep in class, getting lower grades, and cannot pursue after-school activities.... In large urban centers, such as New York and Los Angeles, the problem is more serious. Inspectors have found nineteenth-century-style sweatshops where poor immigrants—young girls of twelve years and above—hold daytime jobs, missing out on school altogether. And a million to a million and a half migrant farmworker children—some as young as three and four years—are at work in the nation's fields. These families cannot survive without the effort of all of their members.[2]

The percent of the non-institutionalized population over sixteen years of age that is in the labor force is called the labor force participation rate. Figure 3-2 shows the rates for women, married women, and teenagers for the period from 1970 to 1991. All show sizable increases over those years, but the largest relative increase

Figure 3-2

Labor Force Participation Rates for Women, Married Women, and Teenagers, 1970–1991

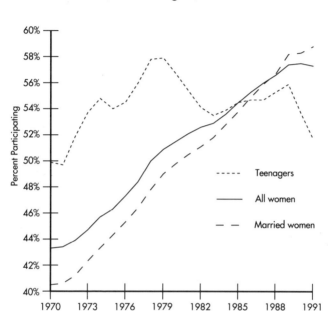

is for married women. In fact, it was the increased work of women that kept family incomes from shrinking.

But all of this extra market work has not been without cost, financial and psychological. When more than one adult in a family works, work-related expenditures increase—for example, child care, clothing, and transportation costs rise. It has been estimated that work-related expenditures are close to 50 percent higher in two-earner families. Further, when family members work more, they are more stressed. According to Schor, "Thirty percent of adults say that they experience high stress nearly every day; even higher numbers report high stress once or twice a week.... Americans are literally working themselves to death—as jobs contribute to heart disease, hypertension, gastric problems, depression, exhaustion, and a variety of other ailments."[3]

Let us examine the hours worked during the period 1979-1989, when the real wage rates of the working class fell most sharply, and consider families in the bottom 60 percent of the family income distribution. Nearly all of these families are what most people would call working-class families, with almost all of their incomes derived from wages (plus government transfers for the bottom one-fifth). The *husbands* in the married-couple-with-children families saw their real yearly incomes fall sharply during this period. However, the real incomes of these *families* either fell by much less or actually increased. Thus while the husbands increased their annual hours (except in the poorest fifth) and there was some growth in the real hourly wage rates of the wives in the second and third fifth (those in the bottom fifth fell), none of this was nearly enough to account for the change in family income. Thus the only conclusion we can reach is that it was increased hours of work by the wives that led family incomes to either rise or to fall less precipitously. Figure 3-3 shows the increase in annual hours of work for all wives in each quintile of the family income distribution for 1979-1989.

These increases in hours are staggering. Consider a family in the second quintile. The average income of all families in this group was $20,746 in 1989 (in 1991 dollars). The husbands in this quintile lost $1.03 per hour in real wages between 1979 and 1989 (again in 1991 dollars). They worked on average 2,138 hours, so the lost income for 1989 was 2,138 times $1.03, or $2,202. In 1989, wives in this quintile had an average hourly wage rate of $6.35. At this rate, to make up for the lost family income caused by the husband's lower real wage rate, the wife would have had to work an additional 347 hours per year, or nearly nine extra weeks ($2,202 divided by $6.35). Fortunately, the wives in the second quintile had higher real hourly wage rates in 1989 than in 1979—$.34 higher to be exact. But if they had worked the same

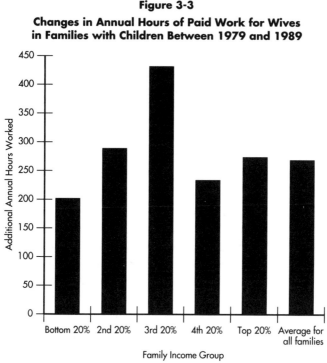

Figure 3-3

Changes in Annual Hours of Paid Work for Wives in Families with Children Between 1979 and 1989

number of hours in 1989 as they did in 1979—which was 708 hours—this higher wage rate would have meant an increase in family income of only $240. It was the many extra hours worked by the wives, along with the small increase in the hours worked by the husbands, that kept the second quintiles' average real income just about the same in 1989 as it had been in 1979.[4]

The downward trend in real hourly wage rates is by no means over. Men's wages continue their long decline, and the increase in women's wages has slowed or, in the case of college graduate entry-level wages, fallen. Hours of work have increased to such a burdensome level that it is hard to imagine that they can continue to rise. According to Schor, "In 1990, one-fourth of all full-time workers spent forty-nine or more hours on the job each week. Of these, almost half were at work sixty hours or more."[5] Furthermore, the added paid employment of women has not been matched by a commensurate decline in work in the household, so that women continue to work a "double day." All in all, the economic future of the working-class family is not a happy one. Unless, of course, working people organize to reshape it.

MULTIPLE JOBS AND OVERTIME

Part of the increase in hours worked is due to the higher labor force participation rates of women and teenagers. However, those already in the labor force have increased their hours of work by working overtime and by taking on more jobs.

According to official statistics, more than 6 percent of employed people hold more than one job, and there was a sharp increase between 1979 and 1989.[6] And it is likely that the percentage is a good deal higher than this, since many second jobs are "off the books" and those holding them may be unwilling to be honest to interviewers. Most of the increase in the multiple job-holding rate was due to economic hardship—that is, "to meet regular household expenses or pay off debts"—as opposed to "saving for the future, getting experience, helping a friend or relative, buying something special, enjoying the work, and so forth."[7] The sharpest increase took place among women, again for reasons of economic distress. By 1989, a higher percentage of women than men were moonlighting because of economic hardship.[8]

While some multiple job-holders combine two or more part-time jobs to get the equivalent of one full-time job, the data on hours of work indicate that most moonlighters work a lot more than the equivalent of one full-time job. In 1989, the average number of hours of work per week for multiple job-holders was 52—55.8 for men and 47.1 for women. Fourteen percent of all such workers labored more than 70 hours per week, equivalent to about two full-time jobs.[9]

Like multiple job-holding, overtime has risen dramatically, driven both by its appeal to cost-cutting businesses and to needy workers. To quote Juliet Schor again, "Among manufacturing employees, paid overtime hours rose substantially after the recession [of the early 1980s] and, by the end of 1987 accounted for the equivalent of an additional five weeks of work per year."[10] The United Auto Workers union estimated that in 1988 overtime work allowed for a reduction of the workforce by 88,000 union brothers and sisters.[11]

COLLEGE PROFESSORS AND AUTOWORKERS   Two examples from my personal experience illustrate the circumstances leading to multiple job-holding and overtime. Due to a divorce and remarriage, I found myself financially strapped. To make ends meet, I took on several other jobs: moonlighting at other schools, consulting for attorneys, and doing labor arbitrations. My own school faced budget difficulties and found it cheaper to offer overload courses instead of hiring new teachers. This saved the school the cost of recruiting new teachers, as well as certain fringe benefits and payroll taxes. We were a perfect match. Other teachers, whose wages had not kept pace with inflation, did the same thing, so that now about one-quarter of the college's classes are taught on an overtime basis. Of course, the quality of the classes suffers and I am burned out, but such is the nature of the system. A couple of aspirins, some antacids, a few drinks, and I'll be like new again.

I sometimes have occasion to teach groups of autoworkers at a local factory. Most of them are skilled tool-and-die makers, with hourly wage rates of at least

$20. Three years ago there were about 2,000 employees at the plant; today there are 900. Yet overtime is endemic. A few workers make nearly $80,000 a year. If a worker labored for 2,080 hours (52 weeks times 40 hours) at $20 an hour, he would earn $41,600. To reach $80,000, he would have to work an additional 1,280 hours at time-and-a-half overtime pay of $30 per hour. This averages out to a staggering 64.6 hours per week. Again, it is cheaper for the company to push overtime (in fact, it can demand it) rather than hire new workers: costly benefits do not rise and no training or hiring costs have to be paid. And the workers are not always unwilling victims of corporate greed. Like me, they are trapped in the cycle of what Juliet Schor calls "work and spend." They have financial commitments and they have bought into the idea that happiness equals consumption at least equal to that of your neighbors. At some plants workers have voted to keep the overtime rather than spread out the work so that more workers can be recalled from layoffs.

OUT OF HIGH-PAYING INDUSTRIES AND INTO THE SERVICE SECTOR

The trends in wages and hours documented above are closely connected to changes in the nation's industrial and occupational structures. The changes in the industrial structure are well known. When I was growing up, manufacturing was the heart of the economy. Automobiles, steel, rubber, glass, electrical equipment: these were the industries that were identified with the U.S. economy. These industries were heavily unionized and therefore paid the highest wages and provided the best benefits. They also helped to set the standard for other industries, where employers had to worry that their workers would unionize or leave for the higher paying union jobs.

Today U.S. manufacturing is a shadow of its former self. Thousands of plants have been closed, many of them relocating to low-wage havens in the South and abroad. Existing facilities have aggressively downsized, lopping off hundreds of thousands of workers, including many management personnel. Figure 3-4, which looks at the basic trends in employment by industry, shows clearly that the major growth is in the sector of the economy that produces services rather than goods. Retail trade and services (business services, such as janitorial work, health services, and personnel services) increased their share from 35.8 percent to 42.8 percent, a gain of 7 percent. This may not sound like much, but it accounted for 79.7 percent of all the growth in industrial employment during the decade. On the other hand, manufacturing lost 5.3 percent of its share, or 1,644,000 workers.[12]

The hard fact is that the industries that are shrinking pay better and offer more benefits than do those that are expanding. There are many ways to show this. For example, had the industrial structure remained the same in 1989 as it was in 1980, average wages and benefits would have been several percentage points higher. If we look at the average pay in the expanding and the shrinking sectors, we find large and growing differences. During the 1981-1987 period, average compensation (1987=base year) in the contracting sectors was $10,404 more than in the growing sectors, an enormous differential and the highest in the post-World War II era.

Low-paying industries are also the most likely to use the contingent workers described at the beginning of this chapter. According to economists Polly Callaghan and Heidi Hartmann, "Between 1970 and 1990, part-time workers in trade and services increased their share of the total nonagricultural wage and salary workforce from 11 to 14 percent. By 1990 one in seven workers was a part-time worker in trade or services."[13] Contingent workers are less likely to receive fringe benefits than full-time permanent workers, and this increases the compensation gap between the expanding and shrinking industrial sectors.

Figure 3-4
Employment Shares by Industry, 1979 and 1989

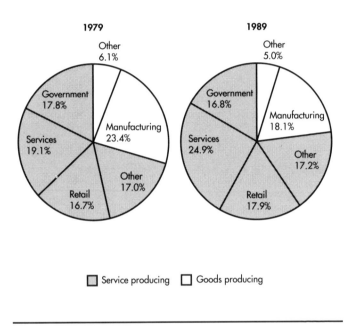

1979

Other
6.1%

Government
17.8%

Manufacturing
23.4%

Services
19.1%

Other
17.0%

Retail
16.7%

1989

Other
5.0%

Government
16.8%

Manufacturing
18.1%

Services
24.9%

Other
17.2%

Retail
17.9%

☐ Service producing   ☐ Goods producing

The growing industrial sectors are less unionized than the declining sectors, which also lowers average wage rates. It is well documented that unions mean higher wages and fringe benefits: in 1989, for instance, there was a "union premium" of $7.06 per hour in total compensation for blue-collar workers.[14] In four contracting industries (manufacturing, mining, construction and transportation, and public utilities) in 1988, unionized workers made up 22.1, 18.7, 21.1, and 33.1 percent of all workers, respectively. In three expanding industries (wholesale and retail trade, services, and finance, insurance, and real estate), the percentages were 6.7, 5.9, and 3.5, respectively.[15]

CHANGING OCCUPATIONS

While it is clear that the shift toward service-producing indus-tries has pushed working-class incomes downward, the effect of the changing structure of actual jobs is not so clear-cut. Much has been made of the increase in the number of high-skill, technical jobs that require considerably more numerical skills, as well as computer literacy, than is possessed by the average labor force entrant. An oft-cited report, *Workforce 2000*, prepared by the Hudson Institute for the Department of Labor, argues:

> The jobs created between 1987 and 2000 will be substantially different from those in existence today. A number of jobs in the least-skilled job classes will disappear while high-skilled profes-sions will grow rapidly. Overall, the skill mix of the economy will be moving rapidly upscale, with most new jobs demanding more education and higher levels of language, math, and reasoning skills.[16]

This argument will not withstand careful scrutiny. First, these new jobs make up a very small fraction of total employment, and their growth in the future will not appreciably raise their share of the job pool. In fact, the *Workforce 2000* report admits that by the year 2000 the five most highly skilled occupational groups will include a mere 6.1 percent of all jobs.[17] Second, the increase in the number of skilled jobs has already slowed down from the growth rate of the 1970s and 1980s, and it is estimated that occupational shifts between now and the year 2000 will add very little to real wages or to average skill requirements for the econ-omy as a whole. Third, the next decade or so will also see considerable growth in certain low-skill jobs. A recent report of the Economic Policy Institute states that "it is the service occu-pations, dominated by low-skill occupations such as cooks, wait-ers, household workers, janitors, security guards, and the like that will make the *largest* contribution to total employment growth between 1984 and 2000."[18] This shift will put downward pressure on overall skill and real wage levels.

THE GREAT TRAINING FIASCO   The best analyses available give little hope that there will soon be an explosion of high-skill, high-tech jobs. Yet a centerpiece of Clinton administration economic policy is job training: if only the poorly trained youth of today could learn how to read and write better, use computers, and master some technical skills, the economic and social catastrophes that have struck the working class will be mere memories of a period of hard but necessary adjustments to the more competitive international economic environment—or so the argument goes. Unfortunately, this thinking puts the cart before the horse. Good jobs will not be created simply because workers are more skilled. They will only be created if the jobs that require them are created. As economist Robert Pollin has put it, "The Pentagon provided the foundation for the postwar development of the aerospace, communications, and electronics industries—the most successful U.S. industries over this period, both as technological innovators and as exporters. They flourished because the Pentagon offered research and development subsidies, guaranteed markets and protection from foreign competition."[19] Now that military spending is being scaled down, the government had better come up with a replacement (Pollin suggests environmental reconversion) if all of the newly trained workers are to have anything worthwhile to do.

UPGRADED JOBS OR THE DEGRADATION OF WORK?

If we grant that industrial and occupational changes have not and will not have an appreciably positive effect on either skills or real wages, it still might be true that there will be an upgrading of *individual* jobs. That is, won't the secretary or janitor of the future (not to mention the technical, scientific, or managerial worker) have to be more skilled than his or her counterpart today? While this is a another commonly held belief, it too cannot be verified by the evidence. For example, it is often asserted that the more mechanized the workplace or the more rapid the technological change, the more skilled the work becomes. But as Harry Braverman and others have shown, the correlation between mechanization and the skill content of jobs is often negative.[20] At best, there is no necessary relationship between technological progress and skill upgrading.[21]

The issue of the skill content of jobs is usually associated with the management techniques pioneered by the Japanese and now widespread in the United States. The new workplace is characterized by close cooperation between management and labor. Employees work in semi-autonomous teams, trained to solve all types of workplace problems, whether of a technical or personnel nature. The prototype workplace is the New United Motors Manufacturing Incorporated (NUMMI) plant operated by General Motors and Toyota in Fremont, California. According to company public relations handouts, workers there are not the drones who slaved on the assembly lines but multi-skilled team members, cooperating with management to produce a quality automobile at a reasonable price.

Those few students of "total quality management" (as it is called by its propagandists) who have taken the time to analyze it critically have renamed it "management by stress."[22] First of all, the content of the work is rigorously time-and-motion studied, with techniques that the founder of "scientific management," Frederick Taylor, would have envied. This pre-planning of the work removes most skills, so that it is now possible for each team member to master a variety of "jobs," none of which has much skill to it. The teams are pressured relentlessly to improve productivity: in fact, the pace of the work is often so fast that only young workers can keep up. There are no relief workers, so the teams hate absentees. No inventory is available to cover glitches along the line. All of this has nothing whatever to do with skill.

What is important to the company is that workers have the right attitude toward work and the company. When the auto plants hire, they are far more concerned with the applicant's past absentee record and union activity than they are with his or her skills.

JUNK JOBS

There is one final matter to discuss, and that is the nature of the employer-employee relationship. This too is undergoing a profound change. As full-time, long-term jobs become a thing of the past, employment has become part-time, temporary, and insecure. There are five main types of what we have called contingent workers: involuntary part-time workers, temporary workers, leased employees, homeworkers, and "independent" contractors. Let's take a brief look at each.

As the next chapter will show, there has been a sharp increase in the number of employees who want and need full-time work but can find only part-time employment. Here we note that part-time workers earn less money per hour than full-time workers—$5.06 compared to $8.09 in 1990.[23] Further, the lower pay of part-timers lowers the pay of full-timers in those industries with a high concentration of part-time workers. Few part-timers are unionized—only 6.7 percent in 1989—and therefore few have fringe benefits. For instance, less than 15 percent of part-time workers have employer-provided health insurance. Those part-timers with some health insurance seldom have coverage for their dependents. The growth in involuntary part-time and other contingent work is one of the reasons for the rapid increase in uninsured Americans.

What is true for medical benefits is also true for other fringes, such as pensions. The low wages and absence of benefits force many part-timers to apply for public assistance and Medicaid. Polly Callaghan and Heidi Hartmann report, "In 1990 more than 1.6 million people received government assistance because they could not obtain full-time work."[24] This represents one-third of

CF-062292-C

all involuntary part-time workers. In addition, involuntary part-time employees are less likely to qualify for unemployment compensation or to be protected by the panoply of worker protection legislation, such as workers' compensation and occupational health and safety laws. Naturally, the rate of poverty is much higher among these workers than among their full-time brothers and sisters.

There have always been help agencies that find workers for businesses on a temporary basis (e.g., Kelly "girls"), that is, for some specified period of time, usually a few days, weeks, or months. Recently, though, the use of "temps" has boomed, growing three times faster than total employment since 1982. In 1990, there were 1.3 million people employed by firms using agencies in the Help Supply Services Industry (HSSI) and probably many more hired directly by employers (one estimate is as high as 18 million). Temps, like part-timers (temps can also be part-timers, of course), earn less money and have even more meager benefits. Average hourly earnings in 1990 for HSSI workers was $8.08, compared to $10.03 for all nonsupervisory and production workers. For temporary office clerks and construction laborers, the wage rates were considerably less than this average. Only 23 percent of temporary workers have major medical insurance even partly paid for by the employer, and only 37 percent received paid holidays. Temporary workers are disproportionately women (more than 60 percent), which helps perpetuate male-female wage differentials.

Temporary employment is becoming a more normal and long-term business practice. In the past, temporary work increased as the economy grew and shrank as the economy slumped. Now it has become much less cyclical:

> If temporary work is being used in a less cyclical fashion, then temporary work may increasingly be being built into business as usual. Such a possibility raises the further possibility that temporary work may be displacing what would otherwise be permanent jobs. The use of contract labor to substitute for regular workers, not only as a way to avoid long-term commitments, wage growth, and substantial fringe benefits, but also ... as a way to avoid occupational safety and health protections, is especially disturbing.[25]

Amazingly, the government itself has also become a major user of temporary workers: there were 300,000 temporary employees in the federal sector in 1988.[26]

The firms that use part-time and temporary workers act as their employers. With leased employees, however, the employer is the company that leases them. For example, the college in which I work once contracted with the Wackenhut Company to supply the campus police force. The police were employees of Wackenhut, not the college. We assumed that the college paid enough to cover wages plus some fringe benefits, but we learned later that the company pocketed the fringes and paid only the wages. In recent years, some firms have fired entire categories of employees and then leased them back, like pieces of equipment, from the leasing company that hired them after they were dis-

charged. They do exactly the same work as before, but their former employer now has no responsibility for them, even though it will continue to describe their work responsibilities and discipline them. In such circumstances, it is difficult for workers to know who is responsible for maintaining legal standards or with whom to try to negotiate higher wages. Not surprisingly, it has proven very difficult for unions to organize leased employees.

Homework is the fourth form of contingent work, and is as old as capitalism itself. Under the "putting-out system," a merchant-capitalist provided a weaver—to use a classic example—with raw wool and perhaps a loom. The weaver and his family would then work up the wool into cloth and be paid by the piece when the weaver returned it to the capitalist. This system was extremely exploitative. The capitalists used competition among the large pool of unorganized and isolated weavers to beat down their wages, forcing them into destitution so great that they had to send their six- and seven-year-old children out to work in the newly built factories. Such arrangements were also common in the garment industry early in this century, when thousands of women and children brought cloth home to make dresses, coats, and suits.

Organized labor was able to force the federal government to outlaw homework in seven industries in the 1940s. Unfortunately, the economic reversals endured by workers in recent decades, most especially by newly arrived immigrants from poor countries like El Salvador, China, and the Philippines, have led to a resurgence of this most debased kind of labor. A 1981 survey found 50,000 illegal homeworkers in New York City alone.[27] The Reagan and Bush administrations championed homework and refused to enforce laws against it, arguing that it is a good way for women to make money and still be at home with their children. The fact that these women often earn much less than the minimum wage, work killing hours, and get no benefits does not seem to faze these noted promoters of "family values."

Homework has spread from its traditional havens in the clothing industry to insurance, electronics, and even automobiles. With computer technology, workers can do clerical work at home on computer terminals monitored automatically by management. Homeworkers in the insurance industry need not necessarily even be in the same country as the employer. One almost unbelievable example of homework is described by Philip Mattera:

> The new homework is not limited to the cities. Companies like General Motors have literally begun to farm out subassembly work to rural workers in the Midwest. In Iowa, farm wives like Sarah Johnson put together front-end suspension components for GM cars, earning piece-work wages that often amount to only a few dollars an hour. "The worst part," Johnson told a reporter, "is that the work is always there waiting for you. On Sundays. On holidays. It's there when you get up in the morning. And after you're through farming at night. There's just no turning it off. I'm sure they're taking advantage of us. I mean, *somebody* was getting paid a lot of money to do this in Detroit."[28]

The last category of contingent work is independent contracting. There are legitimate independent contractors—self-employed people such as accountants and freelance writers. However, this category has expanded far beyond what would normally be expected as firms have declared their employees to be contractors, thus avoiding social security and unemployment insurance taxes. This is exactly what happened to one of my nieces. She was working for a small furniture store whose owner was in financial difficulty. He persuaded each of his sales people to sign agreements converting them into independent contractors, responsible for their own work-related expenses. Such ruses have become so common that the IRS has begun to investigate independent contractors with only one client (their former employer). In nearly all cases, it has found the arrangement to be fraudulent.[29] Most of the guilty employers will not be caught, of course, so we can expect this abuse to expand even further in the future.

4

UNEMPLOYMENT

WHAT SHOULD WE EXPECT?

We are often told that we live in the best and the richest country in the world. It is certainly true that the United States is a rich nation. We are blessed with vast supplies of natural resources and a large labor force. Combined with millions of machines, tools, and factory buildings, these produce the world's largest output. Our total yearly production, excluding what are called intermediate goods and services (such as the steel that goes into automobiles), is now in excess of $5.5 trillion dollars. This amounts to over $20,000 in annual output per person each year, or $80,000 for a family of four!

Not only does our economy produce a lot, but it has achieved amazing increases in output over a very short period. Probably the best example comes from World War II. Between 1939 and 1944, output nearly doubled, a feat all the more remarkable when we remember that millions of working men and women left their workplaces to enter the armed forces. New factories were built and old ones were retooled to produce war goods.

Given that our economy is so productive, what should we expect from it? What do we have a right to expect in terms of living standards? No doubt each of us would draw up a different wish list, but I think many people would agree with the following, spelled out by President Franklin Roosevelt in his 1944 State of the Union address:

1. *The right to a job*. Surely in a country as rich as ours, every person who wants to work ought to have a job. And not just any job, but one that pays a living wage for a reasonable number of hours and does not force us to risk life and limb to do so.

2. *The right to decent housing*. Perhaps we cannot supply a house to each family unit, but we certainly ought to be able to ensure that no one is homeless.

3. *The right to a good education*, an education that helps us fulfill our potential in all spheres of life, from the economic to the artistic to the political.

4. *The right to adequate health care*, both in terms of prevention and treatment of injury and disease.

5. *The right to be free from the economic fears of unemployment, accident, sickness, and old age.*[1]

All of these rights are interconnected—the achievement of one rests on the achievement of all the others. But in the United States rights (2) through (5) all depend on the attainment of the first right—a job. Without steady and reasonably well-paid work, we run into all sorts of trouble. If my father had not had a good job, I would not have had good health care. Nor would I have been able to go to college. We would not have been able to afford a decent home, and our home life would probably have been more troubled. My father would not now have an adequate pension (or any pension at all), and the illness from which he suffers would have killed him long ago.

Compared to many, my father has been lucky. While most

people in the United States believe that every person willing to work ought to have access to a job, we certainly do not enjoy a right to employment, let alone a job that pays enough to support a family. For at least the last hundred years, unemployment has been a chronic problem, both in the United States and in Europe. It has left in its wake a host of social troubles and threatened the peaceful slumbers of those who are working.

UNEMPLOYMENT IN THE UNITED STATES

While unemployment is an old problem, it was not until this century that the government accepted any responsibility for eliminating it, or that most economists admitted that it had anything to do with the nature of our economic system. Throughout the eighteenth and nineteenth centuries, those in power, and those who spoke and wrote on behalf of the powerful, agreed that some people were unable to work and that these people deserved at least some public assistance. On the other hand, they also argued that those able to work but *unwilling* to do so should not be given anything so that their laziness would not be encouraged and others would not be tempted to imitate them. Both the Western European countries and the United States invented a host of devices to force the "undeserving" poor to work, from branding their bodies to putting them in prisons and workhouses, from making their children wards of the state to prohibiting them from begging.[2]

None of these punitive schemes put much of a dent in the number of unemployed, although they did help to create a powerful public prejudice against them. It was true that some people chose not to work, but the conditions inside most early workplaces were so horrible that it is hard to blame them for choosing begging or the dole.[3] In fact, these voluntarily unemployed might better be seen as rebels against the new industrial economy that was sweeping away older, more personal, and less "clock-driven" cultures of work.[4] The harsh treatment meted out by the poor

laws and workhouses tells us just how bad work was in industri-
alizing Europe and the United States. The unemployed had to be
punished so that the employed would stay at work.

But not all beggars and tramps were unemployed by choice,
while the unemployed were not all beggars and tramps. At any
given time there were many thousands of people who desperately
wanted to work but could not find jobs. When the economy went
into a slump or a depression, the ranks of the involuntarily
unemployed swelled enormously. And these depressions occurred with such regularity in the nineteenth century that it
became apparent that they were an essential part of the capitalist
economy. When factories shut their gates because there was no
demand for their products, it was difficult to say that those
thrown into the streets had *chosen* to become unemployed. Fear-
ing that these unemployed men and women, who couldn't be
considered beggars and tramps, might cause trouble, governments began to consider less punitive ways to deal with them.
Many suggestions were made, and some programs were begun.

COUNTING THE UNEMPLOYED

Every month, the Bureau of Labor Statistics (in the Department of Labor) and the Bureau of the Census conduct a survey
of 65,000 "households" to determine how many people are unemployed. These households are enumerated in a census of
households that the government conducts every ten years and
regularly updates. A household is basically the space in which
people live, whether in traditional families, in a group of unre-
lated persons, alone, etc. People living in various "institutions,"
such as prisons, mental hospitals, and group homes, do not live
in households and so are excluded from the count. However,
members of the armed forces are included. The 65,000 households are chosen from the population of all households in a more
or less random procedure—in other words, each household has
the same chance of being surveyed. Once the households are

selected, surveyors go and ask questions about labor market activity. The survey is always taken during the week that includes the twelfth day of the month.[5]

On the basis of the answers to the survey, household members are placed in one of three categories: *employed, unemployed,* and *not in the labor force.* To be counted as a member of the labor force, a person must be at least sixteen years old, so those under sixteen are never in the labor force (even if they are working). The government uses the following definitions for each category:

Employed. To be counted as employed, a person must be sixteen or older and must have either worked at least one hour for pay in the previous week *or* have worked at least fifteen hours without pay in a "family" business *or* have held a regular job but did not work due to illness, bad weather, temporary leave, strike, lockout, etc. Note that the definition of employed makes no distinction between full-time and part-time work. Note too that if you meet the definition of employed, you are placed in this category regardless of what else you did. For example, if you worked on Monday but were laid off on Tuesday and spent the rest of the week looking for work, you are classified as employed for the entire month.

Unemployed. To be counted as unemployed, a person must be at least sixteen, must not be employed, and must have either actively looked for work within the past four weeks *or* be on temporary layoff *or* be waiting to start a job within the next month. A person can look for work by registering at a public or private employment office, answering a job ad, sending out resumes, going for job interviews, registering at a union hiring hall or professional registry, etc.

Not in the labor force. All those who are neither employed nor unemployed are placed in this category. Remember that those less than sixteen go here no matter what their labor market activities. This is important because child labor is on the increase, but many working children do not show up as employed. Also, until 1994, all women who told the surveyors that they were full-time homemakers went into this category without further questioning. This meant that homemakers looking for market work were not counted as unemployed, as they should have been. Correcting for this error will add to the female unemployment rate.

If we add together the total number of employed and unemployed, we get the "labor force." The unemployment rate is then calculated by taking the number of unemployed and dividing it by the labor force. This decimal fraction is multiplied by 100 to get the rate of unemployment as a percent. For example, suppose that there were 950 employed persons, 75 unemployed persons, and 500 persons not in the labor force. The labor force is 950 plus 75, or 1025. The unemployment rate is 75 divided by 1025, or .073, which multiplied by 100 gives us 7.3 percent. Here is the formula:

$$950 + 75 = 1025$$
$$75 / 1025 = .073$$
$$.073 \times 100 = 7.3\%$$

At present in the United States, the labor force is about 125 million people, so that each percentage point of unemployment equal about 1.25 million unemployed. An unemployment rate of 7.3 percent means that means that 9.125 million people are unemployed.

KEEPING THE UNEMPLOYMENT RATE LOW It is important to understand that defining unemployment is a political act: a "generous" definition will help to shape our attitudes about our economic system in ways different than a "stingy" one. For instance, as we shall see later, the definitions of employed and unemployed lead to a serious undercount of the number of unemployed. In addition, the Bureau of Labor Statistics has made changes over the years that have further lowered the unemploy-

**ment rate. (No change was ever made that increased it!)
First, since the early 1980s the armed forces have been
included as part of the labor force, reducing the unemployment rate because soldiers are by definition employed. Second, in 1967, the period in which a person
had to have looked for work to be counted as unemployed was cut from 60 to 28 days, which also reduced
the number of unemployed. Third, people on strike used
to be counted as unemployed if they looked for work
while on strike, but this is no longer the case: now they
are counted as employed for the duration of the strike.**

UNEMPLOYMENT RATES IN THE UNITED STATES

Figure 4-1 shows the unemployment rate by year since 1890.
The rates are for the civilian labor force—the armed forces are
excluded—in order to make the figures for past years comparable
with those in recent years. There are many interesting things to
note about these data. First, they move in a pattern, several years
of increase followed by several years of decrease. This is because
a capitalist economy moves in cycles of prosperity and depression. Many things have changed during this century-long period,
but not the ups and downs of the business cycle.

Second, unemployment rates in the period since World War
II have not moved up and down as much as they did before the
war. For instance, we have not had an official unemployment rate
above 10 percent since 1940, while the rate was in double digits
sixteen times before that. The most important change in our
economy since 1940 has been the enormously increased role of
the government. For instance, in 1929, the last year of prosperity
before the Great Depression, government expenditure on output
as a percentage of total output (Gross National Product, or GNP)
was about 8.3 percent, but in the middle of the 1980s it was about
24 percent.[6] During World War II, the government bought nearly

Figure 4-1
Unemployment Rates, 1890–1993

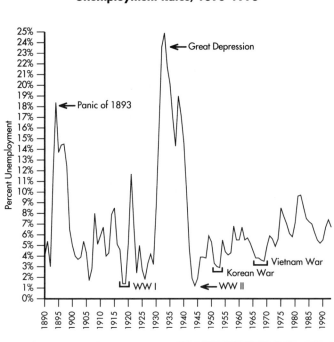

50 percent of the economy's output, one of the factors that brought the Depression to an end.[7] After the war, the government did not reduce its buying, and this, along with a variety of what are called government transfer payments (unemployment compensation, social security benefits, public assistance, etc.), have helped prevent another depression. Conservatives tell us that government spending is the cause of our current economic problems, but history tells us that without it we would have been back in trouble long ago.

Third, our economy has seldom generated full employment.

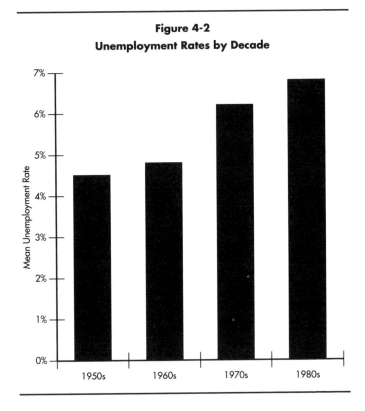

Figure 4-2
Unemployment Rates by Decade

At any time some people are unemployed: they may be looking
for their first job, re-entering the labor market after an absence,
or quitting one job and searching for another. Even if there were
enough jobs to go around, it would take time for the unemployed
to find them and in the meantime they would be unemployed.
Such unemployment is called *frictional unemployment* because it
involves mismatches or friction between the available job open-
ings and the unemployed. The question is, how low can the
frictional unemployment rate can be? In other words, how low is
it possible to get the unemployment rate under normal economic
circumstances? While some capitalist economies have been able

to keep their rates below 2 percent over extended periods of time, most economists believe that this is too low a rate to hope for in an economy as large and complex as ours. Leaving aside the truth of this argument, let us suppose for now that such low rates are impossible except in times of extreme labor shortage (such as World War II). What then would the lowest rate be?

When I first began to study economics, in 1963, the President's Council of Economic Advisors said that we should strive for an unemployment rate of 3 percent. Later, when I was in graduate school, a less optimistic council said that 4 percent was the best we could do. Still later, the Reagan and Bush councils argued that 5.5 percent was the equivalent of full employment. Let us use each of these "full employment" rates and compare them with the actual rates in Figure 4-1. But first note that for all 104 years between 1890 and 1993, the *mean* unemployment rate (calculated by adding the 104 rates and dividing by 1043) was 6.86 percent. The *median* rate, which is the rate such that 50 percent of all the rates are equal to or below it and 50 percent are equal to or above it, was 5.5 percent. The lowest rate was 1.2 percent and the highest was 24.9 percent.

In fact, we achieved a rate of 3 percent or less only 13 times, and more than half of these (7) were war years. Even using the much higher Reagan/Bush rate of 5.5 percent, we achieved that standard in only 55 of the 104 years—in 49 years, or nearly half of the time, the rate has been over 5.5 percent. If this is the best we can do, then we are in a lot of trouble.

A final but critical point is that the unemployment rate has been steadily rising since World War II. Figure 4-2 shows that the mean (or average) unemployment rates has risen in every decade since the war, and by a whopping 64 percent over the four decades. Even during the 1980s—a period that included the longest peacetime expansion in our history (1983 to 1989)—unemployment averaged 7.15 percent, or about 8.9 million people. This was the result of what Reagan called "the magic of the marketplace." Some magic!

> **MINORITIES AND UNEMPLOYMENT** Unemployment af-
> fects minorities more than whites. The unemployment
> rate for blacks is typically double that for whites, while
> the unemployment rate for black teenagers seldom falls
> below 30 percent. The rate for Hispanics is also much
> higher than for whites. In the depression year of 1982,
> for example, the rates for whites, blacks, and Hispanics
> were 8.6 percent, 18.9 percent, and 13.8 percent respec-
> tively. While blacks are not over-represented in part-
> time employment, they are more likely than whites to be
> discouraged workers.[8]

THE HIDDEN UNEMPLOYED

These statistics show an economy that has persistently failed
to use its labor force, and one that fails more and more often. And
yet these statistics *undercount* the true amount of unemployment,
because they do not include what we can call the "hidden unemployed." Consider again the government's definition of employed: to be counted as employed, a person only has to work *one
hour* for pay in the preceding week. No distinction is made
between full- and part-time work. Yet part-time work is defined
as less than thirty-five hours per week and is a growing proportion of all work. For example, in February 1993 the Bureau of
Labor Statistics estimated that employment grew by 380,000
while the unemployment rate fell by 0.1 percent. Conservatives
in Congress argued that this improvement demonstrated that
President Clinton's jobs program was unnecessary. But of these
380,000 jobs, 348,000—84 percent—were part-time.[9]

Some people work part-time by choice—perhaps because they
have other responsibilities that make full-time work impossible
or undesirable. Many others, however, work part-time because
they cannot find full-time jobs or because their hours have been
cut back. These workers are called "involuntary" part-time work-

ers. All told, there are more than 5 million involuntary part-time workers in the labor force today, and the number continues to grow.[10] As more companies rely on part-time and temporary workers, both to lower their costs and to forestall unionization, the number of involuntary part-time workers has increased. Between 1970 and 1990, total employment grew by 54 percent, while involuntary part-time employment grew by 121 percent. Involuntary part-time workers made up 3.1 percent of the total workforce in 1970 and 4.5 percent in 1990—a 45 percent increase.

When people want and need to work full-time in order to survive but can only find part-time jobs, it is legitimate to consider them *partially unemployed.* The Bureau of Labor Statistics surveyors, although they keep track of involuntary part-time employment, still count it as employment. But if two workers whose hours are cut from 35 to 17.5 per week are counted as part *un*employed, they would be the equivalent of one unemployed person—rather than two fully employed people, as they are now. In other words, each involuntary part-time worker would count as a fraction of an unemployed person rather than as a whole employed person. Adding all these fractions would give us the total unemployment accounted for by the involuntarily unemployed. This would of course lead to a big increase in the unemployment rate.

A second type of hidden unemployment results from the definition of unemployed. Remember, to be counted as unemployed a person must have actively looked for work within the past four weeks. When that person stops looking for work, he or she is classified as a "discouraged worker" and put in the category "not in the labor force."

Why do people stop looking for work? Are they unwilling to work? No. We know that people are willing to work when work is available: if they weren't, there would be many more jobs waiting to be filled. The trouble is that jobs are not always available. Consider this example: In 1982 I was living in Johnstown, Pennsylvania, which for the previous hundred years had been a center of steel production. The depression that struck the nation in 1982 had a devastating effect on the local steel industry. Thousands of long-term steelworkers were laid off, with little chance of being recalled. The Johnstown area led the nation in unemployment for several months, with rates reaching nearly 30 percent. In such an economy, how likely is it that a middle-aged steelworker will find employment? Few employers were willing to hire these older workers, especially those used to making good money in a union setting. As the costs of searching for a job (transportation, food, clothing, etc.) mounted, many people decided that the costs were much greater than the benefits (none) of looking for work. These people stopped the job search and got by as best they could. But when they stopped looking, they were no longer counted as unemployed—despite the obvious fact that they would take work if it were available.

The Bureau of Labor Statistics also keeps track of discouraged workers, but again they are not counted as unemployed. Thus the unemployment rate actually *falls* when unemployed people stop seeking work! For example, suppose that the labor force consists of 900 employed and 100 unemployed people, giving us an unemployment rate of 10 percent. Now suppose that all 100 of the unemployed stop looking for work: the labor force would decrease to 900, the number of officially unemployed would drop to zero, and the unemployment rate would drop to 0 percent. But would this mean that the economy was performing well?

The number of discouraged workers depends on the definition used, but by the Bureau's own conservative count there were nearly 1 million discouraged workers in any given month in 1993. Their numbers increase during economic downturns. This means that the official unemployment rate increasingly understates unemployment as the economy's performance worsens.

Figure 4-4

Official Unemployment Rate by Race-Ethnicity and Sex, 1980–1991

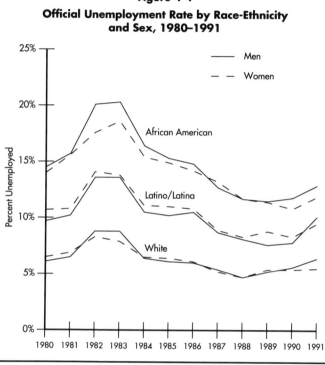

A TRUER UNEMPLOYMENT RATE

By adding involuntary part-time workers and discouraged workers to the "officially" unemployed, we can arrive at an expanded unemployment rate, which is a more accurate measure of unemployment. As we noted above, the Bureau of Labor Statistics keeps track of a variety of unemployment rates besides the one that is usually reported by the media, including both discouraged *and* involuntary part-time workers. Figure 4-3 compares the expanded and official rates for the years 1967 to 1993.

In 1982, a year of severe economic crisis, the official rate was

9.7 percent, the highest since the end of the Great Depression. In other words, officially more than 10.5 million people were (on average) unemployed each month in that year. If we look at the expanded rate, however, we see the actual unemployment rate was far greater, a whopping 14 percent, or more than 15 million people. Imagine if the expanded rate had been reported in the newspapers and on TV every month. Imagine if the TV commentators made these numbers the subject of their columns and commentaries as often as they did, say, the treacheries of Saddam Hussein. Do you think that the public's attitudes toward the Reagan administration might have changed? Do you think that if the true rate of unemployment was publicized month-in and month-out, people would begin to think that it was a pity that the richest nation in the world cannot provide 15 million people with jobs?

As we have seen, the number of hidden unemployed has been rising faster than the number of officially unemployed, mainly because of the increase in involuntary part-time workers. This means, as Figure 4-3 shows, that the gap between the official rate and the "true" rate is widening. For example, in 1973, the official unemployment rate was 4.9 percent, the lowest rate for the decade. This was 70 percent of the true rate of 7 percent. In 1988, however, the official rate was 5.5 percent—again the lowest rate for the decade—but this was only 65 percent of the true rate of 8.4 percent. As the number of full-time, year-round jobs continues to shrink, this gap will continue to widen, making the official rate of unemployment an increasingly unreliable indicator of the performance of the economy. For instance, during the recession years of 1991 and 1992, the official unemployment rate did not rise to the level reached during the 1982-1983 recession, despite the fact that many commentators considered it to be every bit as severe as the earlier one. This anomaly is explained in part by the fact that in the most recent downturn much of the unemployment was hidden and therefore did not show up in the official statistics.

WASTED OUTPUT

If we look at unemployment at the most basic level, we can see that it is profoundly irrational from a societal point of view. For most of human history we lived as gatherers and hunters, moving in small groups from place to place, hunting animals and gathering berries, seeds, and plants. We were attached to our land and tools in the sense that there was no group of people who could deny us the right to use them. If we were hungry and food was available, we would work to get it. We could not be unemployed. We might not work because we had just eaten, but no one could tell us that we could not work when we were hungry as long as animals were there to be hunted and roots and berries to be gathered.

Suppose that we could transport a group of hunter/gatherers to the United States in 1933. They would see something very strange indeed. On the one hand, they would see idle land (and mines, mills, and factories), land that could be used to produce food. And on the other hand, they would see idle human beings, hungry, in rags, and without shelter, human beings willing and able to produce food, clothing, and shelter—and obviously in need of them. They would certainly think that they were in a land of crazy people, a land in which people could produce the food, clothing, and housing they needed but were not doing so. What a waste!

Of course, what differentiates us from hunter/gatherers is that we do not have the *right* to use the land and factories because they are private property. They belong to a small number of people and can be used by the rest of us only with their permission. Such an arrangement means that there will be unemployment if the owners decide not to let us use their property. When, as sometimes happens, this refusal occurs on a large scale, millions of people are thrown out of work, the land and factories are allowed to stand idle, and the waste of output reaches astounding proportions. The Great Depression of the 1930s is a good example. In 1929, the last year of the prosperous 1920s, businesses were operating at 83 percent of capacity; in other words, only 17 percent of their productive capacity was idle. The official unemployment rate was 3.2 percent. By 1932, however, businesses were operating at only 42 percent of capacity (in some industries, such as steel, the utilization rate was as low as 10 percent), which means that more than half of the country's mines, mills, and factories were idle. The official unemployment rate was 23.6 percent.[11]

The waste of potential output during these years is staggering to contemplate. Suppose that we assume that the nation's output could have grown at a rate of 3 percent a year during the 1930s—not an unreasonable assumption because the Gross National Product has grown at that rate over extended periods of time. Had this happened, output by 1937 would have been nearly 27 percent higher than it was in 1929. Yet in fact it had just barely reached the 1929 level—a measure of the waste of food, clothing, and shelter generated by the widespread unemployment. And these figures understate the goods we might have had because they do not take into consideration the new techniques of production and new products that might have been developed during the 1930s.

WASTED PEOPLE

We normally think of our economy as producing goods and services, but things are more complicated than that. As we work, we not only make useful things, we also make ourselves. Through our work, we become what we are: our work is part of what defines us as human beings. Seen in this light, unemployment takes on added significance. Work is a social experience, one of the main ways in which we connect to our fellow human beings. An unemployed person cannot make these connections and is therefore made to be less than fully human. It should not be surprising, then, that unemployment is a blow to a person's ego, to his or her sense of self-worth. Not only is the output that the

Table 4-1

Some Consequences of Unemployment

Consequence	Predicted Increase over Five Years
Arrests	732,000
Overall mortality	105,000
Prisoners	40,000
Cardiovascular deaths	27,800
Mental hospital patients	9,000
Suicides	1,900
Cirrhosis deaths	1,700
Homicides	1,300

unemployed person could have produced being wasted; the un-employed person is being wasted as well.

While sociologists have long studied how unemployment affects the lives of the unemployed and their families, modern researchers have added a concreteness to the earlier, more impressionistic studies. For instance, Harvey Brenner of Johns Hopkins University has been studying the effects of unemployment for the past twenty years, both in the United States and in England.[12] He uses the same research method used by scientists to demonstrate the effects of cigarette smoking: he chooses two sample groups of people who are alike in every respect but one. In the cigarette studies, the people in one group smoke, while those in the other group do not. In the unemployment studies, the members of one group are unemployed, while those in the other group are not. Differences between the groups can then be attributed to smoking or, in this case, unemployment.

Brenner's studies show that unemployment is an important contributing factor to a wide array of personal and social problems. They also allow him to attach numbers to each of these consequences of unemployment. His most recent study, which examined the effects of the increase in unemployment between 1989 and 1990, predicted the effects of this increase over the next five years. Table 4-1 summarizes his findings. For instance, Brenner predicts that the rise in the unemployment rate between 1989 and 1990 will lead to 732,000 *more* arrests over the next five years (1990-1995) than would have occurred had the rate of unemployment remained the same. The reason is that as people lose their jobs or cannot find work, they are more likely to do things or be in places that increase the chances that they will be arrested. And, as the table indicates, some of those arrested will end up in prison—40,000 to be exact. No wonder that as unemployment rates have risen since the 1950s, the United States has come to lead the world in the number of people in prison. No wonder that prison construction has become a growth industry, with poor communities across the nation competing with one another to be chosen as the site for each new prison. Who can be surprised that, with unemployment rates in black communities often exceeding 50 percent, young black men are more likely to be in jail than in college?[13]

Needless to say, unemployment affects more than the unemployed. Brenner found that the members of an unemployed person's family were more likely to suffer mental and physical impairments than were family members in households that did not experience unemployment. Unemployment leads to stress within families, which in turn makes spouse and child abuse more likely and creates an environment in which divorce is often the outcome. In addition, unemployment forces the larger society to spend money for health care, prisons, and a variety of social services which it would not have to spend in the absence of unemployment. This raises the question of prevention: would it not be better for society to practice "preventive medicine" by insuring full employment in the first place?

If it is true that unemployment makes people physically and mentally sick, and if it is true that unemployment helps keep our prisons overflowing, then it must also be true that some of the people in hospitals and prisons should be counted as unemployed. Like discouraged workers, these people have also dropped out of the labor force because of depressed economic conditions. At present there are more than 1 million people in prisons and mental hospitals.[14] Between 1989 and 1990 the prison population rose by about 50,000. Brenner estimated that the increase in unemployment from 1989 to 1990 led to 8,000 more prisoners, or 16 percent of the total increase. If we used this as a crude measure of the hidden unemployed in our various institutions, we would have to add at least 160,000 people (16 percent of 1 million) to the total unemployed. More important, though, is for us to realize that many people in prison, in mental institutions, and on the streets are not there because of some genetic defect or personal neurosis but because our society cannot or will not provide enough jobs to go around.

KILLING US SOFTLY As we shall see, the federal government can reduce or increase the amount of unemployment through fiscal and monetary policies. Given the tremendous social costs of unemployment, a thoughtful person might therefore ask why the government would ever choose to increase unemployment. Here is one possible scenario.

No one can doubt that large banks and financial institutions have great economic power and that this economic power translates into political power. The president's economic advisors are usually drawn from Wall Street, and there is no reason to believe that the advice given by these financiers will be harmful to their former employers. What the banks want is low inflation, because rising prices reduce the value of the loans they make. Suppose that our economy experiences greater than average inflation, as it did during the late 1970s and early 1980s. The financial community will then put pressure on the government to enact policies that will reduce inflation, from cutting government spending to increasing taxes. Monetary policies will push interest rates up. All of these measures will reduce spending, which will in turn reduce sales. Firms will lay off workers and these newly unemployed people will be forced to cut their spending, reducing both sales and employment still further. As the downturn deepens, wage costs will decrease and there will be less pressure on firms to raise their prices. *In other words, unemployment will cure inflation.*

Unfortunately, it will also kill workers: the steeper the rise in unemployment, the more people will die. Looked at this way, the policies of Presidents Carter and Reagan between 1979 and 1982—policies consciously aimed at creating unemployment in order to stop inflation—can be seen as acts of murder. These policies were all the more heinous when we consider that they were accompanied by deep cuts in the social programs that would have softened unemployment's blows.

THE NEED FOR FULL EMPLOYMENT

The U.S. national anthem calls this the land of the free. And it is true that on paper we have a wide variety of freedoms—the fabled freedoms of speech, press, and religion. However, we also have the freedom to be unemployed, and throughout our history this has been a freedom exercised by all too many people. It is

Figure 4-3
Official and Expanded Unemployment Rates, 1967–1993

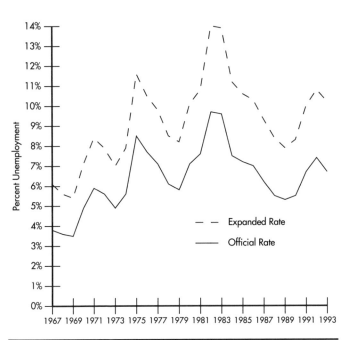

hard to see how the unemployed can enjoy their constitutional rights. In a society such as ours, the lack of a job and the concomitant absence of an income almost negates our formal freedoms because unemployment condemns us to poverty, poor health, and low self-esteem. Our presidents harp on human rights, but what about that most basic of all human rights, the right to do what only human beings are capable of doing, namely, to work? A nation that denies its people the right to work is as guilty of violating human rights as a nation that puts people in prison without trial. What makes this human rights violation especially intolerable is that we are fully capable of producing full employment—we did so during World War II. The fact that we have not done so all the time is a great injustice, one that should make us burn with anger.

Compounding the inequity of unemployment is the fact that it is not distributed evenly among the various social groups that make up the nation (see Figure 4-4). How can we be surprised at the disproportionate number of young black men and women among our poor and homeless and in our prisons when the unemployment rate among black teenagers is at Great Depression levels? Even during the great Reagan boom, the unemployment rate among black teenagers never fell below 32 percent—7 percent higher than the rate for the entire nation at the height of the Great Depression. For Hispanics, the rate during this period never went below 22 percent.[15] And remember, these are official rates: the expanded rates are even higher. A full employment policy, guaranteeing a job to anyone who wants one, would be a civil rights achievement of great importance. President Clinton talks about training the poor and the unemployed so that our country can compete in the world market. He should be saying that we must provide jobs so that people can live with dignity and in good health, as is their *right.*

Mainstream economists revere efficiency, yet they seldom examine the great waste caused by unemployment. In his excellent but sadly neglected book, *Securing the Right to Employment*, Philip Harvey tells us that there are three costs associated with unemployment.[16] First, we provide some unemployed people with income, in the form of unemployment benefits, food stamps, public assistance, and other similar transfer payments. Between 1977 and 1986, the period of Harvey's study, these cost us $90 billion per year, or about $1,000 per person. Second, we spend billions of dollars to treat the unemployed for the diseases that unemployment causes and to incarcerate them when unemployment leads them to crime. Third, we give up the goods and services that the unemployed would have produced had they been working. Harvey estimated this lost output at $1.2 trillion over the same ten-year period, or about $1,600 per person per year. What sort of logic can justify this staggering waste? My wife and I have four children. Excluding the per person cost of medical care and incarceration, the above figures show that unemployment is costing my family about $13,000 a year!

UNEMPLOYMENT POLICIES IN THE UNITED STATES

Until the Great Depression, the United States had no systematic unemployment policy. Care of the unemployed was left to local and state governments, which seldom acted unless the unemployed themselves became unruly and demanded relief. Private charity, direct public relief, and occasional public works projects were designed to curb the anger of those without work. Such aid was always given grudgingly and with the assumption (often stated outright) that the unemployed were responsible for their own condition. However, during the Great Depression unemployment became so widespread and the unemployed so agitated that it became clear that the government would have to take action. It was therefore during Franklin D. Roosevelt's first administration that the federal unemployment policies still in existence today were put in place.

Aid to the unemployed takes three forms: direct relief, unemployment compensation, and jobs programs. While direct relief—outright transfers of money to the unemployed—was one of the first actions taken by the federal government in 1933, it has never been the preferred policy, and it was a measure of the desperation of the times that it was provided at all. Today, direct relief is controlled by the states and is doled out in tiny amounts. Most of what is called "general assistance" goes to people who are not currently able to work, though they may well be the victims of past unemployment. Relief to "able-bodied" adults is anathema to the government, and general assistance programs are a favorite target of demagogic politicians.

THE EROSION OF GOVERNMENT SUPPORT FOR THE POOR
Those at the bottom of the income distribution pyramid
obtain a substantial part of their income from various
government transfer payments, such as Aid to Families
with Dependent Children (AFDC), food stamps, Medicaid,
housing assistance, etc. These families have faced a double whammy. Not only have their real wage rates fallen,
but the real value of the government transfers has fallen
as well. The real value of the "benefit sum" (equal to
AFDC, food stamps, and Medicare) has fallen about 30
percent since the mid-1970s.[17] Conservatives have argued that welfare was a major reason for the increase
in poverty in the 1980s because women in single-parent
households collected assistance. That this argument is
false is clear from the simple fact that the AFDC participation rates of female-headed families with children actually fell, from 63 percent in 1973 to 42 percent in 1987.[18]

The states also provide Aid to Families with Dependent Children (AFDC), which goes overwhelmingly to women raising
young children on their own. This aid, along with in-kind transfers (such as food stamps and medical assistance), is only given
to those who have no assets and it is given under conditions that
stigmatize the recipients. In addition, many states have enacted
some sort of "workfare" scheme, which forces the women who
receive public assistance to work for their aid or to enroll in
job-training programs. Several appraisals of these "welfare reforms" have shown them to be more concerned with reducing
government expenditures and providing businesses with a pool
of docile low-wage labor than with getting people off the welfare
rolls.[19] In President Clinton's Arkansas, for instance, the only
"trained" welfare mothers who got jobs in one of the state's
poorest counties were employed by the training agency itself.

Meanwhile, the county's numerous unemployed wait hopefully for the building of a new federal prison, which will undoubtedly house some of the rest of the nation's out-of-work millions.[20]

The nation's most ambitious public works programs were also established during the Great Depression. The Civil Works Administration (CWA), which was put in place in six short months in 1933 and 1934, employed 4.3 million people at its peak, while the Works Progress Administration—which lasted from 1935 to 1943—employed almost as many. Immensely popular with working people, who preferred real work at a living wage to relief, the CWA undertook 180,000 projects. And under the WPA:

> More than 650,000 miles of roads were constructed or repaired, along with bridges and viaducts, drainage ditches, culverts, sidewalks, curbs, gutters, traffic lighting and signs, and roadside landscaping. More than 125,000 buildings were built or repaired, almost one-third of which were schools. Others included libraries, auditoriums, gymnasiums, offices, hospitals, penal institutions, dormitories, firehouses, garages, storage facilities, armories, and barns and stables. Almost 3,000 public utility plants were built and another 1,000 upgraded, and telephone and telegraph lines, electric power lines, water mains, water wells, and water storage tanks were installed. More than 2,100 swimming and wading pools were built or improved...[21]

Business leaders hated these programs because they forced private companies to pay wages that equalled those paid by relief programs and because they threatened to give people the radical notion that employment was their right. They were especially despised in the South, where they upset the system of racial discrimination on which the profits of Southern businesses rested.

Since the 1930s, the federal government has made several lukewarm commitments to providing jobs for the unemployed, but actual programs have been limited and the emphasis has been more on training than jobs. The jobs that have been provided through such programs as the Comprehensive Employment and Training Act (CETA) have been easily attacked as "make-work" projects. Reagan and Bush dismantled most of the job programs then in place and put new and greatly reduced programs in the control of the very business interests that oppose any attempt to create public jobs.

THE UNEMPLOYED ORGANIZE The unemployed in the United States have never been a passive mass waiting for help. From the first seamen thrown out of work by a shipping embargo enacted by the government in 1807 to the thousands of workers displaced by plant closings in the 1980s and 1990s, the unemployed have marched, picketed, petitioned city halls and the U.S. Congress, disrupted public meetings and church services, commandeered trains, conducted sit-ins in welfare offices, prevented evictions and foreclosures, formed unions and supported strikes, organized soup kitchens and food banks, established local barter economies, and constructed local, state, and national organizations to fight for their rights.

The most famous unemployed organization was established during the Great Depression, when millions of unemployed formed Unemployed Councils, often led by Communists and Socialists, in cities across the country. These councils demanded immediate help for unemployed men and women from often hostile local relief agencies. By using militant tactics, such as mass sit-ins and demonstrations, they forced the authorities to take their needs into account and to take actions that benefitted them. There is no doubt that this aggressiveness, often in the face of severe repression, helped to alter the political climate and made possible the public works projects, unemployment compensation, and public assistance that were begun in the 1930s and have continued

into the present. There is also no doubt that all recent organizing efforts among the unemployed have used the Depression movement as a model.[22]

The one unemployment program that has remained intact since the Great Depression is unemployment compensation. Billed as an insurance system, it is funded by a payroll tax and run by the states. Since the payroll tax can be partly shifted onto workers and consumers, this system in effect makes workers pay for the support of the unemployed. To qualify, an unemployed person must have worked in a job covered by compensation and must have earned a certain minimum amount during a specified period. Benefits are not available to first-time job seekers or to those re-entering the labor force. Benefits vary greatly from state to state, but seldom reach even half of full-time earnings. The basic assumption is that unemployment is a short-term phenomenon, so benefits are usually available for no more than twenty-six weeks.

While clearly inadequate as a cure for unemployment, unemployment compensation does provide those out of work with some money to keep body and soul together. It means that those who lose their jobs do not have to take the first offer that comes along. This greatly irritates employers, because it helps keep wage rates up. Some economists have gone so far as to argue that unemployment compensation helps keep unemployment rates artificially high because it allows people to wait before accepting work. These sorts of arguments gave the Reagan/Bush administrations all the ammunition they needed to undermine the unemployment insurance system: eligibility requirements were tightened and benefits reduced to the point that unemployment compensation can no longer be considered a safety net for a majority of the unemployed. For example, during the severe recession year of 1975, 76 percent of the unemployed received unemployment benefits. By contrast, in the depressed year of

1991, only 42 percent got benefits. In fourteen states, fewer than 33 percent of the jobless received compensation, and in three states the proportion was less than 25 percent. To make matters worse, during 1991 a record number of unemployed exhausted their benefits without qualifying for more aid. President Bush repeatedly vetoed the supplemental aid that had been provided by Congress in previous recessions and only agreed to support it when his popularity in the opinion polls plummeted and threatened his re-election bid.[23]

No matter how bad unemployment gets, there will still be many more employed than unemployed. Many of the employed may figure that their chances of losing their jobs are fairly remote, and they may not see themselves as the natural allies of the unemployed. Yet we have already seen that unemployment is a social problem that affects *all* working people by wasting output and leading to many social problems. The assault on the unemployed and the poor under Reagan and Bush did incalculable damage to *all* working people. The more porous the "safety net," the more willing the unemployed are to take the jobs of those who are now working. As the corrupt public utilities capitalist Samuel Insull put it, "My experience is that the greatest aid to efficiency of labor is a long line of men waiting at the gate."[24] It is not an accident that the reduction in public assistance to the unemployed and poor during the 1980s corresponded with the precipitous decline in union membership and major losses in real wages and fringe benefits described in Chapters 2 and 3.

THE FEASIBILITY OF FULL EMPLOYMENT

Our unemployment record is not a very good one, but could it have been any better? Could we realistically have had public policies that kept unemployment significantly lower? Or would such policies have been prohibitively expensive and caused other, equally serious, problems?

There is no question that unemployment can be reduced by

political means. The two basic methods, both of which trace their roots back to the work of the British economist John Maynard Keynes, are fiscal and monetary policy. Fiscal policy uses the government's taxing and spending powers to stimulate the economy. The basic idea is that for the economy to get out of a depression, more must be spent on goods and services. The trouble is that the consumers and business firms that spend money on food, housing, machinery, and so on hesitate to spend more in a depression or recession. If a business makes an investment (purchases a machine, for example) and the economy does not revive, it will not make a profit on its investment. If the investment is a large one, the failure may mean bankruptcy. Therefore, the reasoning goes, it might be wiser not to make the investment until the economy recovers. On the other hand, unless such investments are made, the economy will never recover. In such a situation, the government can intervene in the following manner: by transferring to *itself* the money that private businesses and individuals were not going to spend (i.e., their savings) and then spending it on goods and services. Such a transfer can take place by taxing private savings or by borrowing them. The government can take this transferred money and spend it on hospitals, schools, roads, and bridges, stimulating the economy this way. The more spending, the more output produced and the more jobs created.

The second method that the government can use to stimulate the economy is monetary policy. We have in place a system of federal reserve banks, directed by a Board of Governors, which implements monetary policy. (The governors are appointed by the President for fourteen-year terms—the current chairperson is Alan Greenspan.) The complex workings of this system are beyond the scope of this book, but the basic idea is to make it easier for private firms and consumers to borrow money in times of depression. This is done by increasing the amount of funds that the private banks have to lend: it is assumed that if banks have more money to lend, they will lower the interest rates they

charge borrowers, and these lower rates will encourage more borrowing and spending. The increased spending will then create jobs.

The trouble with both monetary and fiscal policy is that they typically depend on "appropriate" responses from the private sector. But lower interest rates do not in fact guarantee more borrowing: if my job is not secure, I may not buy a house no matter how far interest rates have fallen. Furthermore, money borrowed at low interest rates may not be spent productively: it may be used to finance investment in low-wage economies like Mexico, or it may be used to buy other firms, as in the buyouts financed by debt in the 1980s. Similarly, government spending may swell corporate profits rather than increase output and employment. Just look at the defense boondoggles and the savings-and-loan bailout. Generally speaking, private businesses are interested in profits and cannot be relied upon to respond to government stimuli in ways that will guarantee employment.

And in fact our unemployment record since the end of World War II shows clearly that fiscal and monetary policies have not succeeded in maintaining full employment. However, there is no reason why the government cannot keep the economy at full employment *directly* by providing public employment to all those who want it. There are innumerable jobs that the unemployed could do, jobs that would fill important social needs. This was shown to be true by the CWA and WPA in the 1930s, and it would be equally true today. There are millions of children who need day care, hundreds of thousands of housing units that need to be made habitable, thousands of bridges and miles of railroad track that need to be repaired—just to name a few things that the unemployed could do now or could be trained to do in the future.

In his book, Philip Harvey asks what it would cost for the federal government to guarantee employment to every person who wants it. He assumes that these federally provided jobs would pay a wage equivalent to the "poverty level of income" and that the jobs program would replace most of the unemployment compensation and welfare systems. Using data from 1977 to 1986, years that include the deep recession of the early 1980s, he concludes that the net cost (excluding the savings deriving from the social costs of unemployment, such as increased prison admissions) of guaranteeing full employment over this period would have been $217.8 billion. The price tag to taxpayers would have been significantly lower if the government had not cut welfare and unemployment compensation programs so severely during these years. By comparison, it may ultimately take $500 billion to bail out the savings-and-loan banks. Who can seriously doubt that people doing productive and socially useful work would do more for the nation's economic health than will a bailout scheme that will hand over billions of dollars to people who are already rich, many of whom ran the banks into the ground in the first place? Harvey calculates that the entire program could have been funded by a less than 1 percentage point increase in the social security payroll tax now paid by employers and workers.[25]

UNEMPLOYMENT IS A WORLDWIDE PROBLEM The troubles facing workers in the United States are not unique. Working people everywhere are seeing their real wages fall and their chances of becoming unemployed increase. As capital has become more mobile because of advances in technology, it can move from country to country in search of lower costs. This globalization of capital pits the workers of one country against the workers of every other country, creating the conditions for a free fall in their living standards.

Thus unemployment in Europe is much higher than in the United States, averaging over 12 percent. Worldwide, it is estimated that there are 700 million unemployed. While workers are better organized in parts of Europe than they are in the United States and therefore better able to defend their wages, hours, and working conditions, they have also begun to suffer an erosion of their wages and benefits. Governments throughout the world have slashed social welfare programs, and this trend is likely to continue.

Conditions are far worse among the immigrant groups who do Europe's dirty work. Anti-immigrant sentiment has escalated into riots and brutality in France and Germany, as foreigners have been scapegoated as the cause of economic stagnation. Needless to say, if we look at the countries from which these immigrants have come, in Asia, Africa, and the former Soviet-bloc nations, the situation of working people can only be described as catastrophic. In many countries, the average working-class person subsists on a diet guaranteed to lead to malnutrition.[26]

CONCLUSION

Unemployment is a disease that has stalked the U.S. economy ever since it began to take on its modern form. As we have seen, unemployment robs people not only of their right to live in minimal comfort but also of their self-esteem and mental health. If we judge our society by its unemployment rate, we must give it a failing grade: only during times of total war has the rate been where it should, and could, be all of the time. Today, we are in a period of rising joblessness greater than at any time since the Great Depression. Young people have little hope of secure employment, and minority youth particularly can count on many spells of unemployment in their lives. Yet, as we have seen, having a job is hardly a guarantee of the good life. Falling real wages, more hours, fewer benefits, poorer working conditions, a continuing shift away from manufacturing into low-wage and low-skill services, management by stress, and growing insecurity will be the lot of most new entrants into the labor force. The question is—why? What are the causes of the twin problems of unemployment and deteriorating employment? We must know the causes if we are to propose the solutions, and it is to the causes that we now turn.

5

THE NATURE OF THE BEAST

CAPITALISM IS THE NAME OF THE SYSTEM

The reasons for the depressing trends examined in the last three chapters are seldom discussed in any but the most superficial ways. It is assumed that the economic system is "fundamentally sound"—to use one of the favorite cliches of the rich and powerful during the early years of the Great Depression. "Outside forces" (an oil crisis, natural disasters, the government, the Japanese) or human failings (an unwillingness to work hard, sexual promiscuity, even genetic defects) are the culprits when things go wrong. In much commentary, the economic system becomes an alien being, beyond human control: the best we can do is adapt to it, whatever this might entail in terms of human misery. Everyone faces the same uncontrollable market conditions, and everyone has the same chance of success or failure. Thus we hear the President tell us that we must sacrifice so that the economy can "grow," so we can reduce the deficit, so we can meet the dictates of a new international order. Widespread and growing unemployment are never caused by *political* decisions made by and for the benefit of those with the power to make such decisions.

One of the clearest indications of our economic muddleheadedness is our unwillingness to call our economic system by its name—capitalism—and to know just what this term means. We say we have a "free enterprise" system or a "free market" economy—yet very few people are "free" to start a business, and markets are always bound up in a host of regulations and controls. The essential features of any economic system—the social relationships that people enter into as they produce and distribute a society's goods and services—are hidden by these terms, and we should avoid them if we want to understand what is really going on.[1]

Capitalism can best be described in terms of the two most important groups within it—those who own the society's productive wealth (its land, minerals, mines, mills, shopping malls, etc.) and those who work for them. The first group we call capitalists. They have organized a vast network of multinational business firms, including banks and other financial institutions, which gives them tremendous power. Quite often, this power is linked to the government, in both direct and indirect ways, so that economic dominance is translated into political dominance. The biggest capitalists and the firms they control are our society's prime movers; it is their decisions that shape our daily lives.

Put simply, the goal of the owners is to make money, as much of it as possible, now and forever. Put more formally, their objective is to accumulate capital—to make maximum profits and to use these profits to make their capital grow. Each firm is forced to accumulate because its competitors will overwhelm it if it does not. The great German economist Karl Marx analyzed this accumulation process through his famous letter formula: M-C-C'M'.[2] Each firm begins with a sum of money (M) called money capital. It places this money in the marketplace to purchase the means of production (land, labor, tools, machines, etc.) necessary to make the firm's products; these means of production are called commodity capital (C). Once these inputs have been purchased, the firm must see to it that they are combined in order for production to occur. This combining takes place *inside* the workplace under the direction of the firm's managers. The result is output for sale (C')—for example, steel, cars, computers, banking services, etc. Finally, the firm must return to the market and try to sell the output. If the process is successful, the money obtained from the sales of output (M') is larger than the initial outlay (M). The whole sequence is repeated endlessly, with at least part of the profits (M' minus M) reinvested so that capital growth takes place.

The ceaseless accumulation of capital makes capitalism potentially very productive. New products and technical innovations are always being introduced so that more money can be made. However, there is a major contradiction that plagues the accumulation process. This contradiction takes the form of the working classes, the men and women who actually perform the work that produces the output. What distinguishes workers from capitalists is that they do not own any means of production and have no automatic access to them. A serf in feudal Europe might have been poor, but his family had the right to use a plot of land, simply by virtue of being born on the manor. But for workers to live under capitalism, they must find firms willing to purchase their ability to work—their labor power. This means that if they want to work, they must accept the employer's terms. The inequality in this arrangement allows firms to exploit workers—to get them to work longer than would be necessary if all they wanted was to live adequately. This extra work generates extra output, which in turn generates profits when it is sold.

Of course, workers are not generally happy to be exploited. As they gained an understanding of their situation, they began to organize to limit the exploitation, or even end it altogether. They formed labor unions to improve their wages, hours, and working conditions. They formed political organizations to win reforms or to challenge the system. And the owners were quick to respond—since what benefits workers, other things being equal, hurts owners. The workplace, and sometimes the entire society, have become battlegrounds, scenes of struggle between capital and labor. But the economic and political power that come from owning society's productive wealth give the owners a great advantage in this struggle. For instance, they use both the legal system and brute force (their own and that of the government) to crush the workers' organizations. They also propagandize against the workers' political organizations, often aided by allies in the media and in government, so that workers' parties are branded as "radical" or "communist," and therefore not to be trusted.[3]

The owners take many of the most important initiatives inside the workplaces. Because the interests of the workers and the owners are fundamentally opposed, the owners try to structure the workplace so that the workers have as little room for independent action as possible. Over the history of capitalism, many managerial techniques have been used to control what economists call the labor process. First, workers were herded into factories, replacing the homeworkers who had labored in their homes on materials supplied by the capitalists. Factory work was set at a steady pace; the hours of work were determined by the owners; and the workers were watched as they worked.

This ability to observe proved critical at the next level of control. By noting that skilled workers typically break their work into several relatively simple steps, the managers hit upon the idea of assigning unskilled workers to do each of the steps repetitively—this would be their *only* job. Eventually it became possible to replace most of the manual steps with machines. This detailed division of labor into small pieces and the mechanization that accompanied it had two important effects on working people. On the one hand, by simplifying the work they forced down the wages of more skilled workers, whose services were no longer needed as much. On the other hand, they greatly increased the pool of potential workers because so many more people could now do any given job.[4]

The pool of potential workers is called the "reserve army of labor." Its first members were the women and young children who were forced by the need to earn money (or by the authorities, who recruited them from poor houses and prisons) to work in the new factories and who were able to do so because the work required so few skills.[5] Modern capitalism, through its use of advanced computer technology and "Japanese-style" management techniques discussed in Chapter 3, has vastly expanded the reserve army to include almost everyone who is not now employed. For instance, it is possible to produce automobile engines, once the work of well-paid workers in the United States, using relatively unskilled Mexican labor and highly sophisticated computer-driven machinery. And communications technology has made capital more mobile than ever, able and willing to move across the globe in search of the best places to make a profit.

The reserve army of labor is a feature of normally functioning capitalism. It includes the officially unemployed, discouraged workers, involuntary part-time employees, and all other potential workers (for example, the homemakers drawn into the workforce during World War II). Its basic function is to force workers to accept lower wages, longer hours, and poorer conditions by threatening them with being replaced by someone in the reserve army. With a large reserve army, profits can be maintained and accumulation can proceed.

Because the reserve army of labor serves business in this way, unemployment and low wages are normal features of the economy. And as long as business exerts the primary pressure on the government, a full-employment, high-wage economic policy is unlikely, even if it is fiscally feasible and socially desirable. A government that tried to maintain full employment would soon become the enemy of capitalists, who would use their enormous

power to sabotage it. For instance, they might refuse to open their plants or threaten to move them elsewhere, as happened in Chile in the early 1970s, when Salvador Allende began to implement reforms hostile to capitalists. The government would then be faced with the choice of taking more radical steps to implement its program—such as nationalizing closed plants or prohibiting the transfer of capital out of the country—or capitulating to the owners. The whole history of capitalism gives little hope that the first scenario would be the more likely.

CAPITALISM ACCORDING TO MAINSTREAM ECONOMISTS
According to mainstream economists, which includes nearly all of the economists most of us read in the news-papers or watch on television, the market is the key to understanding capitalism. In the market, buyers and sell-ers make free choices based on self-interest: the capital-ists want profits, the consumers want goods and services, and the workers want jobs. The market gener-ally gives all of these people what they want. When it doesn't, it adjusts to correct the situation. For example, if the market is putting out a low quality good, consumers will not buy it, forcing the suppliers to improve the qual-ity or go out of business. Or if the market is supplying dangerous jobs, workers will not take them, forcing the suppliers of such jobs to offer higher wages, make the jobs less dangerous, or go out of business. As Adam Smith put it more than two hundred years ago, an "invis-ible hand" guides the market so that it produces socially desirable results.

It is important to see that mainstream economists make a critical assumption when they describe markets in this way. They assume that the buyers and sellers meet as *equals*, as "free" human beings who make ratio-nal choices in their own interests. In other words, noth-ing forces anyone to buy a product or take a job. Mainstream economists call capitalism the "free enter-prise" system because they believe that under this sys-tem people are free to make the most basic economic choices. Anything that interferes with this free choice is therefore bad because it denies freedom. For example, they are opposed to minimum-wage laws because they interfere with the "freedom" of the buyers and sellers in the labor market: they cannot buy labor below the mini-mum wage, even though this may be above the worker's productivity, and they prevent a willing worker from selling his or her labor at a wage below the minimum. Both buyers and sellers therefore lose some of their freedom and the society suffers from unnecessary unemployment.

A similar argument can be made about tariffs on foreign imports. These cheat consumers by making them pay higher prices. They cheat workers in this country because they reduce the amount of our products that foreigners can buy. "Free" trade and "free" markets. Just let the markets operate without interference, say these economists, and we will all be well served.[6] As a rule of thumb, working people can make the following assumption about mainstream economists: If a policy seems to be in your interests, the mainstream economist will be against it!

CRISES

Although the accumulation of capital is at the heart of the capitalist system, it does not proceed in an uninterrupted fashion over the long haul. All capitalist economies are prone to crises— periods in which the accumulation process breaks down. During a crisis, unemployment rises and the conditions of the employed deteriorate. And what happens during a crisis generally sets the stage for the next wave of capital accumulation.

Crises are set in motion in a variety of ways, and their severity depends on specific historical circumstances that cannot be predicted in advance. But in general, if accumulation is proceeding rapidly, forces will come into play that will bring economic expansion to an end. First, the reserve army of labor will become depleted as available workers become actual workers. Wages will rise as labor shortages appear. Union membership may increase, and existing unions will bargain more aggressively for higher wages and benefits. Inside the workplace, the struggle between labor and management will shift in favor of the worker. Workers will begin to take longer breaks and will be less easy to browbeat into a faster pace. Absenteeism will rise. But all this will reduce productivity, and this along with rising wages will mean that the employer's unit costs will rise. Some firms may be able to compensate by raising prices, but sooner or later rising costs will lead to lower profits. The lower profits will in turn make business more pessimistic about future profitability and less willing to convert their money-capital into means of production. Business investment and employment will fall, and the downturn will have begun.

During the contraction of the economy, the above forces go into reverse, setting the stage for the next expansion. The reserve army of labor is replenished, wages fall, the employer's power inside the workplace is restored, productivity rises, and unit costs fall. As profit margins are restored, business confidence increases and the upturn begins. Periodic recessions and depressions are, therefore, inherent features of capitalism—as is the reserve army of labor itself. Without them, it is difficult for accumulation to take place.[7]

While the ups and downs of the business cycle are what we might call short-term phenomena, over longer periods of time powerful forces operate to push the capitalist economy into long periods of stagnation.[8] Here the economy is mired in a seemingly endless period of sluggish investment and high unemployment. Periods of expansion are short and weak, and real wages may continue to fall even in an expansion. The key to understanding stagnation is understanding the connection between savings and investment. Savings is money not spent on consumer goods and services, along with money that remains after corporate business firms have paid out all their costs of production. Since savings are not spent, they do not create demand for output, and lack of demand will eventually mean that output will not be produced—firms will not continue to produce what they cannot sell. In order for the demand for output to be maintained, therefore, savings must be converted into spending.

Unfortunately, there is no guarantee that this will happen. And if it does happen, this can be in several possible ways. It might be that business firms are especially optimistic about the future (for whatever reason). This optimism leads them to look favorably on potential investments and to borrow money or use internal funds (or both) to finance these investments. When an investment is made, savings are converted into spending, which is what is needed. Another possibility is that the government transfers unspent savings from the private to the public sector and makes investments itself. It can do this through taxation or borrowing. The taxes would have to be progressive income taxes or corporate profit taxes because working people do not ordinarily save money, so if their taxes increase, they have no choice but to *reduce* their spending on output. Taxing the rich and corporations is another matter. These taxes are paid out of savings, so an increase in government spending is not matched by a fall in private spending.

The government can also borrow the private sector's savings. It can do this by selling bonds, which are very safe investments that pay interest. Of course, only those with extra income will buy them, so they are a good way for the government to get hold of the society's savings. When the government spends the money from the bond sales, there is an increase in spending and output.

While either private or public investment may solve the problem of converting savings into spending, there is no guarantee that this will happen—and strong reasons to believe that it will not. The entire history of capitalism tells us that it is foolish to rely on private investment to solve the problem of slumps. There is no guarantee that private business firms, operating in the unplanned environment of capitalism, will make investment decisions that will boost the economy as a whole. As John Maynard Keynes explained many years ago, when a firm considers making a capital investment, it must look into an uncertain future.[9] For instance, an energy crisis that could not have been predicted turns a previously profitable investment into a loser, or a political upheaval turns what had been a safe haven for U.S. investment into a nightmare of uncertainty. And once uncertainty raises its head, investment declines, expectations about the future become still more uncertain, and investment decreases further. In other words, investment can spiral downward, deepening a depression and overpowering those forces such as lower interest rates and real wages that might have worked to turn the economy around.

Compounding the problem of insufficient investment is the fact that investments may have been made to replace labor and lower wage rates. This can mean that the investment increases the economy's capacity to produce output *at the same time* that it reduces the purchasing power of the masses of people. Under such circumstances, investment cannot continue to increase. It may be possible in the short run to sustain consumer demand through debt, but this cannot be done over the long haul because as interest payments on debt mount, less and less income is left for purchasing new goods and services. Sooner or later the economy must enter a downturn.

An important feature of capitalist economies is a tendency for production to become concentrated in large firms with huge amounts of capital equipment. More productive firms may devour less productive ones, forming oligopolies that have some control of the supply of output, prices, and profits. Firms that have made large capital investments hesitate to replace their capital, even if a better technology is available, because it is so expensive—and they are not under the same competitive pressures to do so.

The growth of large firms in concentrated industries not only dampens the growth of investment but also increases savings: oligopolistic firms make more profits than do smaller, more competitive ones. Thus the economy is faced with a fundamental contradiction: savings rise but investment cannot keep pace. The result is a tendency toward stagnating demand for output, accompanied by high rates of unemployment and stagnant or falling real wages.

Stagnation can be overcome, but it is difficult. For instance, the government can invest enough to stimulate the economy, but this generally occurs only during an all-out mobilization for a war. Under more normal political conditions, the government is constrained by business opposition to public investment, which is seen as a direct competitive threat (for example, cheap public housing threatens private real estate interests) and as a signal to the public that the private sector has failed to meet society's needs and may not deserve its unqualified support. High government spending also weakens the power of business to discipline labor because it keeps unemployment down. Democrats as well as Republicans instinctively shy away from committing the government to an aggressive full employment policy—certainly indirect proof of the political muscle of the owning classes.

If neither private nor public investment can stave off stagnation, what can? History suggests that at times, and in an unpredictable fashion, innovations in production can give rise to investment opportunities that are large enough to counteract stagnation and generate prosperity. In the twentieth century, the greatest of these was the automobile. Once mass-production technology and management had been developed by Henry Ford and others, the price of a car fell to the point at which it acquired a mass market. The manufacture of automobiles required enormous amounts of capital—in the form of land, buildings, and machinery—as well as tremendous amounts of steel, glass, and rubber, and the demand for these spurred investment in all these industries. In addition, cars need oil products to run. And to make them an efficient means of transportation, the government had to invest in building thousands of miles of roads, using billions of dollars of materials and equipment. Finally, cars allowed people to live further away from their places of work and to travel long distances to visit other people and to go on vacations. Suburban housing, motels, gas stations, etc. all owe their existence to the automobile. The capital necessary for all of this literally propelled the economy forward.

The first great "wave of automobilization" occurred during the 1920s. But it could not be sustained, mainly because the incomes of the working class were too low to keep the demand for cars rising. Stagnation overcame growth in the late 1920s, resulting in the most prolonged depression in the history of the nation. The Great Depression was so severe and of such duration that even important mainstream economists began to accept the idea that a capitalist economy had powerful stagnation tendencies built into it. Keynes and some of his followers recommended permanently high levels of public investment and direct government planning of private investment as the only solutions to this dilemma. They argued that this would keep the main features of capitalism intact while at the same time making it palatable to the working-class majority, who were the main victims of the Depression.

THE "AMERICAN CENTURY"

The Keynesian solution was not implemented, however: it was not politically acceptable to capitalists and the labor movement was not strong enough to force its implementation. However, World War II finally brought the Depression to an end. As the editors of the journal *Monthly Review* put it:

> What turned things around of course was World War II. Economically the effects were little short of miraculous: a productive potential previously undreamed of was unlocked. In five years from 1939 to 1944, the country's Gross National Product increased by 75 percent. Unemployment plunged from 19 percent to 1.5 percent of the labor force. And all of this happened at the same time that some 11 million men and women were being mobilized into the armed forces.[10]

Not coincidentally, the federal government's yearly budget

deficit had reached 50 percent of GNP by 1944. Keynes was vindicated, though it took a cataclysmic world war to do it.

After the war there was widespread fear that stagnation would reassert itself. That this did not happen was due to the fortuitous conjuncture of circumstances that gave rise to a quarter-century of economic boom. In fact, this boom was so strong that people forgot the Great Depression and came to believe that rapid growth was the normal state of capitalism. Keynes' far-reaching proposals were ignored, "bastardized,"[11] watered down into the notion that the government could "fine tune" the economy through appropriate fiscal and monetary policies. Some deficit spending and a low-interest-rate monetary policy would make downturns short-lived, and the opposite policies would curb inflation.

The idea of steady growth with little unemployment or inflation proved a pipe dream because the long boom was fueled by special circumstances. Economist Harry Magdoff suggests that five factors that were at work after the war provided the conditions for the boom.[12] First, outside the United States, there was widespread destruction of factories, farms, railroads, power installations, and cities. Rebuilding these spurred an enormous demand for capital, much of which came from the United States. In the United States itself, people earned a lot of money during the war, but could not buy many goods (such as new cars and houses). Household savings therefore increased rapidly and created a pent-up demand. Further, corporations had made large profits during the war and used them to retool for civilian production. And businesses were far more willing to extend credit for the purchase of consumer durables and housing than before the war. This further boosted consumer demand.

Second, Western Europe and Japan enjoyed their first wave of automobilization, and the United States its second. The growth in the use of private automobiles, as noted above, generated a huge demand for all sorts of capital and consumer goods and further stimulated suburbanization, with the associated growth

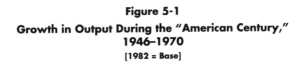

Figure 5-1
Growth in Output During the "American Century,"
1946–1970
[1982 = Base]

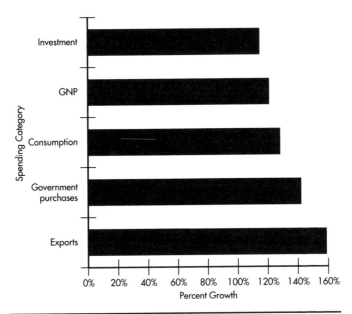

of housing, roads, business establishments, and other car-related services. Third, the war produced significant technological advances, which provided the basis for important new industries, including high-speed jet planes, improved communications, computers, and electronic equipment and devices.

Fourth, and of great consequence, was the decision by the government not to cut its own spending drastically. Domestically, large sums of money were spent on infrastructure (such as roads), and major subsidy programs made it easier for returning veterans to continue their education and to buy homes. The onset of the Cold War, which became an excuse to keep government

spending high and to weaken the labor and progressive movements, was a major component of the demand that kept the
postwar boom going.

Fifth, the United States entered the postwar era as the domi-
nant capitalist country, and our leaders planned carefully to
maintain our dominance. They wanted the United States to
replace Great Britain as the guarantor of political and economic
stability around the world. This "hegemony" would be maintained by a system of treaties and international financial arrangements, ultimately backed by military might. And since the United
States was the only nation capable of supplying the output that
the nations of Europe and Japan needed to rebuild, the demand
for U.S. goods and services abroad remained great. In 1950, for
example, the United States produced 40 percent of the world's
output and nearly all of the nonsocialist world's automobiles,
steel, military goods, and electronic equipment.[13]

During the postwar boom, the United States forced its rivals
to use the dollar as the currency of international trade and
finance. This meant that other nations had to keep large stocks
of dollars on hand to transfer to other countries when their trade
balances were negative. This gave the United States a great advantage because it kept the value of the dollar in terms of other
currencies higher than it would otherwise have been. For U.S.
businesses, the result was that the prices of foreign goods were
kept artificially low, making it much easier for U.S. capital to
penetrate the rest of the world, which it did with enthusiasm.[16] In
addition, trade agreements lowered many trade barriers and led
to an enormous increase in world trade.

The unique U.S. position during this long boom resulted in
significant growth in each of the components of total demand
and, of course, in total output (GNP) and in the real wages of the
majority of working people. This is shown in Figure 5-1. When
we add this to the data on unemployment and employment, it is
clear that the postwar boom was superior to that of the decades
since. Figure 5-2 compares the yearly growth rates of three im-

portant economic variables in the boom years of 1948 to 1973, with those for the following years of stagnation. During the 1980s especially, we see that the pace of output and investment growth slowed markedly, despite the alleged prosperity of the Reagan years.

The labor movement was a force to be reckoned with after the war, one that threatened the plans of the corporate elite for an era of unbridled capital accumulation. The mass-production industries that were the engines of growth were heavily unionized, and many trade union leaders and supporters were political progressives who hoped to extend the radical impulses of the New Deal. On the other hand, U.S. dominance of world capitalism hinged on the suppression of any popular movements for socialism and/or national liberation in Europe or the former European and Japanese colonies. Opposition to the use of force abroad was most likely to come from the labor movement's left wing. Further, businesses did not want working people interfering with the management of the plants: no workplace democracy movements could be tolerated.

The political and business elites therefore mobilized rapidly to contain the labor movement. In the late 1930s, Roosevelt had begun to coopt labor leaders such as Sidney Hillman of the Amalgamated Clothing Workers and Philip Murray of the United Steel Workers, and to distance himself from such potential troublemakers as John L. Lewis of the United Mine Workers. This cooptation process was speeded up by the wartime no-strike pledge and the War Labor Board, on which Hillman and others held prominent, though not decisive, positions. Through such means, business was able to drive a wedge between labor leaders and a strike-prone and militant rank-and-file, and to define certain labor spokespersons as legitimate (which meant inclined toward bureaucratic control) and others as illegitimate (which meant inclined toward control by the membership and often radical, and sometimes Communist, leadership). This business/government labor strategy was strengthened by the Catholic

Figure 5-2
Annual Growth Rates of Real GNP,
Investment, and Productivity

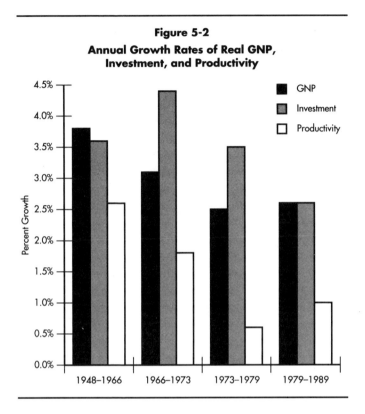

church, which was vociferously anti-Communist and influenced millions of workers and quite a few of the new labor bureaucrats.[14]

The payoff to capital came after the war. The mass strikes that swept the nation in 1946—like the one my father participated in—were not about economic democracy or progressive politics but about bread and butter issues. Inside the unions, war was declared on the radicals. Labor's new "statesmen" capitulated to the draconian provisions of the Taft-Hartley labor law, and later used it to purge the most progressive unions from the labor movement. This law made nearly all types of labor solidarity illegal, from sympathy strikes to picketing to secondary boycotts.

It also demanded that all union officers sign oaths pledging that they were not Communists. Union leaders and large corporations reached an accord in which, in return for unchallenged managerial control, multi-year contracts, and an end to progressive union politics, workers were promised steady real wage and benefit increases. This accord held throughout the long expansion, but, as we shall see below, it actually sowed the seeds of its own (and labor's) destruction.[15]

While the labor/capital accord benefitted union workers, it did little for the majority of nonunion employees and nothing for the poor who were outside the labor force altogether. To help pacify these groups, the government began to increase various types of social welfare spending, such as unemployment compensation, social security, public assistance, education, and health.[16]

THE END OF THE DREAM AND THE CURRENT CRISIS

It is probably impossible to date the end of the American Century precisely. There is no doubt, however, that by the early 1970s all of the forces that had pushed the long expansion forward had lost their sustaining power. The wartime savings were long since spent and the reconversion process completed. Consumer debt continued to grow, but this could not sustain growth over the long run. The world became saturated with automobiles, and demand began to falter, while at the same time Japanese and European competitors cut deeply into the market share of U.S. producers. The result was growing excess capacity in the automobile industry: many more cars could be produced than could be bought. This problem was compounded by the growing awareness that automobile use had serious environmental consequences. The slowing down of car sales removed the most important investment outlet for the growing volume of savings.

Investment spinoffs from defense spending began to peter out. New technological developments in high-tech weaponry and electronics (such as robotics and numerically controlled machines) generated only modest capital spending and actually *decreased* employment opportunities.[17] Defense spending has continued to increase, growing by leaps and bounds during the Reagan/Bush years, but it no longer gives rise to significant investment or employment, at least not enough to overcome the tendency toward stagnation.

Finally, the international power of the United States has deteriorated markedly. Ironically, the rebuilding of Japan and Europe, so important to the earlier dynamism of the U.S. economy, eventually created powerful economic rivals. These competitors used the most modern technology and managerial techniques to produce better consumer and capital goods than U.S. producers. Domestic firms began to lose their markets for a wide range of products. U.S. export growth declined as imports soared, creating deficits in the balance of trade. The military umbrella that the United States had placed over Japan and Europe burdened the U.S. economy, draining away resources and skilled labor (scientists and engineers, for example) from the consumer goods and services demanded by affluent consumers.

The true symbol of the collapse of U.S. hegemony and the end of the American Century was its defeat by the peasant armies of Vietnam. Not only did the war, by flooding the world with dollars, speed up the demise of the world monetary system, but it also placed severe economic and political stresses on U.S. capitalism. The immorality of the war served as a catalyst for all sorts of dissident movements that destroyed the postwar accords so important for capital accumulation. The struggle to end the war inevitably spilled over into struggles against imperialism, racism, sexism, and environmental destruction, and to a profound questioning of the morality of our social system.[18]

When the factors staving off stagnation weakened, profit rates began to fall, marking the start of the crisis. Declining profit rates were followed by the declining rates of growth of the GNP and capital investment shown in Figure 5-2. These fed on one another, generating the stagnation that has characterized our economy ever since.

In response to the crisis of profitability, the business class organized aggressively and collectively, on both economic and political fronts, to restore profit rates. The basic strategy was to cut costs by weakening the already waning power of organized labor and other progressive groups. By the end of the 1970s, capital had decisive advantages in pursuing this strategy. First, rapid technological change and new managerial techniques, both of which deskilled labor, made capital more mobile than ever before. This, along with more favorable tax laws, made it possible for businesses to disperse their operations—both around the country and throughout the world. Plants could be located in isolated rural areas with no trade union tradition and a desperate labor force, or in other countries with wages a fraction of those in the United States and governments all too willing to keep them low. The growing dispersion of capital greatly weakened organized labor. Companies were able to force wages and benefits down by closing plants or threatening to do so.[19] The recently ratified North American Free Trade Agreement (NAFTA) will accelerate these trends through provisions that increase the mobility of capital.

As the crisis deepened, investments in physical capital appeared much too risky. On the other hand, falling real stock prices made existing assets a potential source of higher profits. An orgy of mergers and buyouts ensued, fueled by the invention of new financial instruments, such as junk bonds. As a result, the size of the corporations with which labor had to deal grew enormously:

> In 1960, there were 28 manufacturing corporations with $1 billion or more in assets, representing 27.6 percent of the nation's total manufacturing assets. In 1970, there were 102 billion-dollar corporations controlling 48.8 percent of manufacturing assets. By 1979, 212 manufacturing firms could claim $1 billion or more in assets, representing 60 percent of the nation's manufacturing assets. Billion-dollar firms controlled more of industry's assets, but there were many more such firms.[20]

NAFTA WILL HELP MAKE AMERICA MORE COMPETITIVE

Finally, corporate leaders began to organize politically, not in terms of special interest group organizations but as a unified class with a specific agenda. Taking advantage of organized labor's political weaknesses and its unwillingness to believe that the labor-management accord was over, corporations began to ship money and lobbyists into the political arena on an unprecedented scale. Democrats and Republicans alike, facing no credible opposition to the business agenda, were only too glad to take the money and sing the corporate tune. Business began to get its way during the Carter administration, which appointed the anti-labor Paul Volcker chair of the Board of Governors of the Federal Reserve System. However, it hit its stride during the Reagan years, when the country was literally run by and in the interests of the large corporations.

WHAT'S GOOD FOR GENERAL MOTORS It is an article of faith among the nation's business and political elites that what is good for business is good for the country. As former president of General Motors and Secretary of Defense Charles E. Wilson stated in 1953, "I thought that what was good for our country was good for General Motors and vice versa."[21] Today GM is ruthlessly cutting labor costs by closing scores of plants, moving to low-wage countries like Mexico, and contracting out as much of its work as it can. Like hundreds of other corporations, from USX to IBM, GM will do whatever is needed to restore the bottom line. The consequences of this "restructuring" are there for everyone to see: millions of unemployed, hundreds of towns and communities destroyed, the spread of contingent employment, families in ruin. Just how is all of this good for the country? Only in a country in which people count for so little and money counts for so much could someone say what Wilson said without being howled at with laughter or considered insane. Yet here in the United States, the most educated people believe this propaganda. Oh yes, they wring their hands at the agonies of the suffering masses. But misery today is the price we must pay for prosperity tomorrow. In the face of such nonsense, it is well to remember what economist John Maynard Keynes said about tomorrow: "In the long run we are all dead."

The essence of government policy became helping businesses increase profits by lowering costs. Unions were attacked directly in a variety of ways: Labor law reforms were defeated. The air traffic controllers were fired. Government agencies, such as the National Labor Relations Board and the Occupational Safety and Health Administration, both responsible for guaranteeing the rights of workers, were underfunded and staffed with people hostile to the laws they were sworn to enforce. Employers soon saw that the labor laws would not be enforced or would be interpreted in a pro-business fashion, so they began to ignore them.[22]

The assault on the unions was matched by government help for the corporations and their wealthy owners. The tax system was made more regressive: tax rates for the richest people were cut in half, while those for the majority of workers rose. Corporate tax rates were cut and depreciation allowances made more generous. Businesses were encouraged by tax changes and government bureaucrats to relocate to countries with low wages and repressive governments.

To further discipline working people, the social "safety net" of unemployment compensation, public assistance, food stamps, housing subsidies, and the like was drastically cut. Figure 5-3 shows the overall picture. It is important to note that the main effect was to increase human misery and to make it less likely that those currently employed would take aggressive action against their employers. In other words, the weaker the safety net, the larger the reserve army of labor and the longer capital accumulation can occur without upward pressure on wages.

When Reagan took office in 1981, Volcker had already begun to engineer the worst recession since the 1930s. Under the guise of curbing inflation, the Federal Reserve pushed interest rates up to record levels. Home and car sales plummeted: the steel industry collapsed. The industrial heartland was ripped apart and millions of workers were permanently displaced. Union after union made wage and benefit concessions as the unemployment and employment traumas described in earlier chapters became part of the economic landscape. When the recovery finally came, fueled by massive government debt, military spending, and the remarkable growth of the financial sector, labor was so battered that real wages continued to fall even during the following five-year expansion.

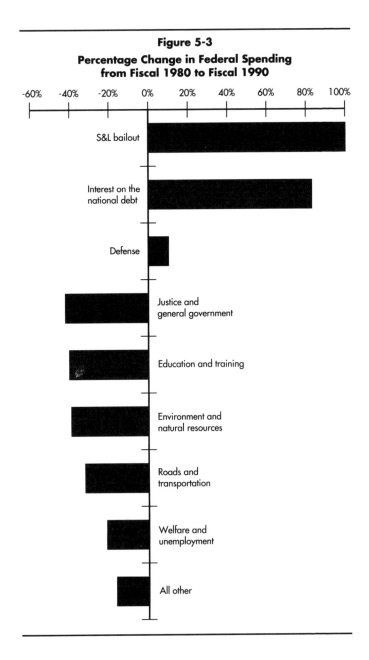

Figure 5-3
**Percentage Change in Federal Spending
from Fiscal 1980 to Fiscal 1990**

While the corporate strategy succeeded in raising profit rates, it could not overcome stagnation. Investment remained too sluggish to sustain high growth rates and plants operated far below capacity. In fact, much of the corporate plan exacerbated stagnation. A low-wage, high-poverty, growing-inequality strategy simply cannot result in a strong demand for goods and services. Of course, our products could be bought by foreigners, but much of the capitalist world was suffering the same stagnation and pursuing the same economic goals. As the 1980s ended, recession had again gripped the economy, and while this last recession has officially been declared over, real recovery is nowhere in sight.

CONCLUSION

The U.S. economy is in the grip of a profound and lengthy crisis. It is difficult for a working person to see a single hopeful sign. Mainstream economists and their political counterparts keep telling us that we are in the midst of an economic restructuring made necessary by inexorable market forces. But the very nature of this restructuring and the political policies that surround it cannot create the conditions for the long-term growth of real wages and employment. In fact, they can only do the opposite. Another World War II is not possible, and no earth-shaking, investment-generating innovations are on the horizon.

The question is—can anything be done?

6

WHAT IS TO BE DONE?

WOULDN'T IT BE NICE?

During the Reagan/Bush years, the rapacity of business reached new heights. Nowhere was the contempt of business leaders for the welfare of the people shown more clearly than in the savings-and-loan scandal.[1] Bank officers looted billions of dollars from banks established to provide working people with low-interest home mortgages, while government regulators turned a blind eye to their machinations. When they were finally caught, the government agreed to bail out these banker-criminals with billions of taxpayer dollars rather than make them pay for their crimes. All told, the bailout's price tag may be close to a half a trillion dollars.

Let us focus our attention upon this staggering amount of money. That's $500,000,000,000, or $500 billion. Now imagine the following alternative use of this money. Hundreds of thousands of men, women, and children are homeless, and millions live in substandard housing.[2] If we define deficient housing as housing "with moderate to severe physical or structural deficiencies," then 17.9 percent of all poor households and 29.2 percent of all poor black households live in substandard housing. Suppose that we concede that half of the $500 billion, or $250 billion, was a necessary use of public funds, but that the other half could be used to build decent apartment buildings and to refurbish existing houses and apartments. In any city, there are thousands of buildings that could be made habitable with little capital and lots of labor. Then assume that half the $250 billion is used for administering the program and training workers in the building trades. For instance, people actually living in the places where the new and rebuilt housing is located could be trained to build their own homes.

This would leave $125 billion for the housing itself. Given that the federal agency that would build the homes does not have to make a profit and can buy supplies at discount prices, the cost of a unit of housing would not be very high. Let's say that the cost of one unit is $50,000. This means that 2.5 million housing units could be built. If four people lived in each unit, all the units together would accommodate 10 million people. In Pittsburgh, which has a population of about 400,000, this housing program could produce enough housing units to house the people in twenty-five Pittsburghs! And we would have thousands of trained workers who could maintain the buildings and build new ones.

My example is overly simple and glosses over a lot of complicating details. However, there is no reason in principle why such a program could not be initiated. Certainly there is a housing crisis. Just take a tour of any poor city neighborhood and see for yourself. Yet what sort of a response would a "war on inadequate housing" elicit in Congress, in the media, and in the business world? It would be met with ridicule, derided as utopian in these hard times. Congresspeople would say that we cannot afford it. Newspaper columnists would rage against a new type of welfare.

Statistics would be put forward to show that there was no housing crisis, that the United States has the best housing stock in the world. Business lobbyists with fat pocketbooks would descend on Washington to scuttle this move toward "socialism." If some bold senator did put forward a bill, it would be DOA—dead on arrival.

Of course, no one in power has suggested such a bold assault on inadequate housing and homelessness. In fact, in the face of this obvious problem, the Reagan administration took steps to deliberately worsen it. As the number of low-income renters rose by 2 million between 1978 and 1989, the supply of federally financed low-rent housing units fell sharply—by a little more than 2 million. New construction of low-income housing units fell from about 500,000 to 100,000 per year between 1977 and 1990.[3]

Housing is just one basic necessity in short supply for a lot of people. There are many others. The Clinton administration has made health care reform a central political issue. It is surely true that health care reform is essential. We have all been made aware of the dismal nature of our health care system, especially for the tens of millions without the means to pay for adequate care: in 1990, 34.4 million people under the age of 65 had no health insurance.[4] Figure 6-1 shows the growth in the number of Americans without insurance over the past fifteen years. Yet the United States spends more on health care than any other nation in the industrial world—a full 3 percent more of Gross Domestic Product than the next most expensive nation (see Figure 6-2).[5] And we rank well down the list of rich nations in life expectancy and infant mortality, two key indicators of well-being. According to Andrew Shapiro, "Black infants in Chicago, Detroit, and Philadelphia have a greater chance of dying within their first year than do infants born in Jamaica, Costa Rica, or Chile."[6] The only doctor's office a poor person is likely to see is the emergency room of an aging and overcrowded city hospital. Literally any working-class family in the country can be wiped out financially by a serious illness.

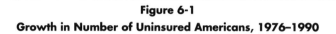

Figure 6-1
Growth in Number of Uninsured Americans, 1976–1990

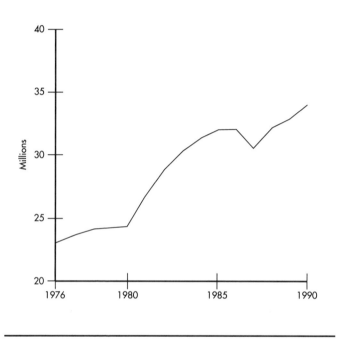

Time and again, people have told pollsters that they favor a single-payer, publicly run system such as the one in Canada.[7] Such a system would be considerably cheaper than the current system and would provide many more people with much better care. Yet the Clinton administration has dismissed a Canadian plan out of hand, and the media acts as if such a system would lead to the end of capitalism as we know it. Instead, Clinton proposes "managed competition," a euphemism for a program that leaves intact the power of the insurance companies and medical professionals, the same groups that drove up costs in the first place. By eliminating the less

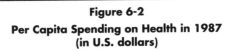

Figure 6-2
Per Capita Spending on Health in 1987
(in U.S. dollars)

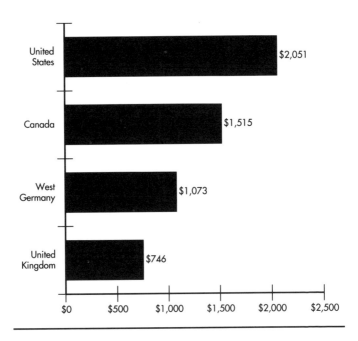

costly and more democratic single-payer plan from consideration, attention can be placed on how costly *any* health care reform program will be and how, in this era of high budget deficits and austerity, we will be lucky if we can get *any* publicly funded care. Yet there is always money to wage war in Iraq or Somalia or Bosnia. When it's a matter of defending the "free world" or America's honor, money can be found, in boundless amounts and on short notice.

In Chapter 4 we examined the problem of unemployment. We saw the costs to working people of the lack of jobs, and how this is part of the nature of capitalism. However, using the research of Philip Harvey, we also concluded that the government could guarantee full employment at a cost nowhere near that of the savings-and-loan bailout. It is hard to imagine that a majority of people in this country would not favor a full-employment policy if it were presented properly and promoted as incessantly as, say, the war on crime. Yet again, we can imagine—because we have already seen—what the response would be to a real war against unemployment. The federal budget deficit would be trotted out to prove that we cannot possibly afford such a "generous" scheme. No one will stop to remind us that, without deficits proportionally far in excess of the current deficit, the Great Depression might never have ended. No one will point out the obvious—that consumer, business, and government debt is essential to a capitalist economy. The important thing to understand about debt is that borrowed money can be used either productively or unproductively.[8] If it is used unproductively to bail out the banks, there will be little economic gain. But if it is used to provide health care and housing, the economy will grow (providing tax revenues to repay the debt) and millions of working people will benefit as well.[9]

The list of problems crying out for solution is long. In 1991, 58.4 percent of women with children under six years old were in the labor force.[10] Their children need affordable, reliable, and nurturing child care. Surely this problem could be easily solved—if there was the will to solve it. It could be an integral part of a full-employment policy and would, in fact, not be very costly in such a context.[11]

We could go on—to the environment, education, drugs, and violence. Make your own list and ask yourself if the problems on it could not be addressed with the money and resolve that the government routinely gives to wasteful and destructive military ventures and to those who are already wealthy. If a polluted environment were made to appear as evil as the Ayatollah

Khomeini or Manuel Noriega, wouldn't we rise up and demand solutions?

IT'S A MATTER OF POWER

People in the United States are cynical about their government. They never tire of complaining about crooked politicians, about deals, about the indifference of the powerful to the plight of the common citizen. Yet at the same time they have given up hope that much can be done. The system is too powerful, the problems too complicated. People are too busy trying to make a living and raise children to have time for politics, and besides, nothing is likely to change even if they get involved.

In this situation, people gravitate toward consumption—in shopping malls, in front of the television, at the sports stadium. Simple-minded answers begin to have an appeal. The religious hucksters tell us that if we get right with the Lord, all will be right with us. Ross Perot's flip charts tell us that the budget deficit is the cause of most of our problems. Demagogues tell us that foreigners are the villains. Don't buy their goods and don't let them into the country and things will get better. This sort of "thinking" shades easily into the notion that there are villains here at home, spreading false doctrines and destroying the values that have been responsible for the country's past greatness. We are told that blacks, feminists, and gays weaken our moral fiber with their poisonous insistence on equality. They must be contained, controlled, maybe destroyed, and then conditions will improve.

In order for working people to begin to understand how their situation might be changed, we have to think about power. Why *doesn't* the government provide adequate housing, health care, and employment? Given that these could be provided by this richest of all countries, the reason can't be that politicians and their expert advisors are ignorant. After all, these people have advanced degrees and successful careers; President Clinton went to Oxford and Yale. It is far more likely that the people in power,

while not omniscient, nevertheless know exactly what they are doing—or at the least know the things they cannot do.

Let us perform a thought experiment. Imagine that in the present-day United States, a truly radical person became President but that nothing else changed (remember, this is a thought experiment!). Imagine too that this President is able to win passage of legislation that commits the government to full employment, universal health care, quality education, guaranteed housing, and so forth. Sharply progressive income taxes and bond sales will be used to finance these programs.

Now imagine how private business would react to this attempt to improve the quality of life of the majority of the population. Most people don't realize that the owners of the largest corporations are well-organized politically. In the 1960s and 1970s, sociologists such as C. Wright Mills and G. William Domhoff showed that there is a class of wealthy people who are tied closely together through their connections to large corporations.[12] These people intermarry, join the same clubs, control most of the largest private charities, serve on the most important government commissions, vote for the same candidates, and share many of the same beliefs. More recent research has shown that the onset of stagnation in the early 1970s forced the rich and powerful to establish still more cohesive organizations, aimed specifically at destroying the power of organized labor and compelling the government to join in their efforts to lower the cost of production and restore profits.[13]

One of the key organizations through which the business elite acts was the Business Roundtable, founded in 1972 and including the leaders of such major corporate giants such as AT&T, General Motors, and Exxon. The Roundtable has been activist from the beginning, building enormous support down to the level of plant managers and supervisors and urging full use of Political Action Committees (PACs) to influence politicians with the one thing they respect—money. The first major success of Roundtable aggressiveness came with the defeat of labor law reform in 1978.[14] With the Presidency and both houses of Congress controlled by the Democratic Party—supposedly the party of labor—the AFL-CIO expected that some fairly mild amendments to the anti-labor Taft-Hartley law would be enacted. But while the unions used professional lobbyists, business sent busloads of plant managers to the Hill to testify against the reforms. Millions of postcards and telephone calls hit Congress and the bill never made it to a vote.[15]

Once our imaginary President has gotten her (it's imaginary, remember) radical plans turned into law, corporate capital will set to work to prevent their implementation. Money will change hands, and before you know it, former supporters will be having second thoughts. And since the plans did not envision any direct attack on the ownership of private businesses, the power that comes from this ownership will be used. It bears repeating that in a capitalist economy, almost everyone depends on the owners of private businesses for survival. In the normal course of events, the power that this dependence gives to private capital is some-what hidden, but in a crisis it would come into the open. Employ-ers would tell their workers in no uncertain terms that the implementation of the President's plan would "force" them to stop accumulating capital.

The owners of our large corporations know that a democratic and progressive set of public policies—the ones needed to ad-dress the problems of unemployment and employment described in this book—are not in their interests. They fight tooth and nail to prevent such options from even being discussed, let alone enacted into programs. In other words, they use their power to get what they want. In our imaginary example, the President's radical programs were somehow magically made into law. But then we jumped back into the real world, which is the world of power. What was missing from the President's progressive plat-form was the power to force it on its enemies.

THE POWER OF THE WORKING CLASS

If one thing is clear, it is that, since the onset of stagnation in the early 1970s, the employed and the unemployed have suffered greatly. Some people have suffered more than others, but the majority has seen its standard of living slide steadily downward. On the other hand, those at the upper end of the income and wealth distributions have prospered as never before (remember Figure 3-1). Mainstream economists talk as if all this was the result of the workings of impersonal market forces. But if this were true, why has capital organized so systematically to influ-ence *politics*—that is, to exert its power? Market forces do not exist in a vacuum but in a social and political environment, subject to the push and pull of power. We know, for example, that market forces, if left to operate without control, have terrible social costs. The market will let a person without money starve to death and an environment be destroyed by toxic pollutants. Market forces are incapable of providing anything close to full employment. If these and many other social problems are to be dealt with, they will therefore have to be dealt with *politically*, in the context of *political* power.

This tells us that an important reason for the decline of working-class living standards must be the absence of working-class power. But before looking at actual working-class power, let us look at *potential* working-class power. We have seen that it is in the nature of a capitalist economy to produce severe problems of employment and unemployment. We have also seen that the essence of capitalism is the exploitative relationship between capitalists and workers—those whose labor is the source of profits and the accumulation of capital. Therefore, an attack on unemployment, on long hours and falling real wages, must in the end be an attack on capitalism, on the capital/labor relationship. It seems obvious that this attack must be waged by the working-class majority, with the help, of course, of whatever allies it can find.

Since workers constitute the majority of the adults in modern capitalist economies, they have great potential power. In a democracy, they have the right to vote. They could form their own political party and run candidates for office. Once elected, these politicians could begin to move the government in a direction that would help the working class. In Sweden, for example, where a party that was at least partly working class in nature has controlled the government for most of the last fifty years, the state has enacted sweeping social welfare legislation, especially in the areas of health care, education, full employment, worker retraining, women's rights, and so forth.[16] While it is true that the Swedish economy remains capitalist and has become mired in stagnation like all of the advanced capitalist economies, the power of Sweden's workers has so far prevented a wholesale dismantling of the welfare state.

But if a working-class political party operated only at the level of electoral politics, it would only have a limited effectiveness. The economy, the source of most people's livelihoods, would still be dominated by those who owned the means of production. The decisions made in thousands of workplaces could negate the gains made in the political arena. Wages could be cut, hours of work increased, workers discharged, and plants relocated or closed. Without a doubt, then, workers must also be organized to exert their power *where they work*. They must form labor unions and federations of labor unions, nationally and internationally, to win some degree of control over their workplaces. They must, through their concerted power to stop working, force their employers to pay them living wages, provide job security, limit their hours of work, and share in the decisions that most affect their lives. This can happen, even during hard times, as our coal miners have shown in their recent struggles against the coal companies.[17]

What working-class political and workplace organizations do is *build class consciousness,* an understanding that working people are capable of thinking and acting in ways that can change their lives for the better. Implicit in the notion of class consciousness is the understanding that worker organizations must have some vision of the future. They must develop a way of thinking about the world that is specifically working class. Given the arguments in this book, this has to mean that working-class organizations must envision, and strive for, an organization of society's means of production that is noncapitalist. For no matter how many reforms are won at work and in the political arena, if the society remains capitalist, the logic of capitalism will always be working to erode these reforms.

Working-class organizations must imagine new ways of organizing production, and when conditions are favorable they must promote their formation. They must give people an expanded vision of what is possible. For example, the U.S. economy is tremendously productive, yet economists continue to say that still greater productivity is needed if our economy is to prosper in the future. From a working-class perspective, this argument is foolish.[18] As productivity rises, fewer workers will be needed to produce any given volume of goods, and the result, especially in this era of stagnation, will be still fewer jobs. Working-class organizations should be fighting for shorter hours with no cut in pay in order to provide more jobs. If a society can produce its output with less labor, this ought to be seen as good rather than catastrophic. Consider this statement from Juliet Schor's *The Overworked American*:

> Since 1948, productivity has failed to rise in only five years. The level of productivity of the U.S. worker has more than doubled. In other words, we could now produce our 1948 standard of living (measured in terms of marketed goods and services) in less than half the time it took in that year. We actually could have chosen the four-hour day. Or a working year of six months. Or, *every worker in the United States could now be taking every other year off from work—with pay.* Incredible as it may sound, this is just the simple arithmetic of productivity growth in operation.[19]

In a society with strong working-class organizations, such responses to productivity growth would be given wide publicity and would be discussed seriously. It would not be taken as some immutable law of the market that people must work longer and harder in an economy with fewer jobs available.

Of course, we must not gloss over the difficulties involved in building working-class organizations. Consider all of the production and nonsupervisory workers in the country, along with all of the people in the reserve army of labor. This "working class" is not a homogeneous mass that automatically has interests in common. There may be divisions between the employed and the unemployed—as, for example, when unemployed workers are used as strikebreakers. Skilled workers may show disdain for their less skilled brothers and sisters, and this may be used to widen the economic gap between them. Male workers may be threatened by female competitors. In fact, work itself is often thought of in masculine terms, as if the labor of women in the workplace and the home is not work.[20]

In many modern capitalist societies, race is a division of major significance within the working class. Not only has work all too often been defined as male, but it has usually been defined as *white* male. In the United States, for example, the racial division was founded in black slavery in the South. White workers based their identities on the fear of becoming like slaves, and used phrases like "wage slavery" to oppose the wage system.[21] After the abolition of slavery, the former slaves were re-enslaved within the labor market and ignored or actively oppressed by the majority of white workers.

Centuries of slavery and racism have left indelible marks on the working class. As late as the 1950s, blacks were constitutionally prohibited from joining some labor unions, while many others simply excluded them as a matter of course. Some strides toward racial equality were made in the large industrial unions that were formed in the crucible of the Great Depression, but these were dashed in the reactionary climate that engulfed the country after the war. Racial inequality was officially sanctioned within the new industrial unions when they agreed to departmental seniority systems, which effectively segregated black workers into the lowest paying and least safe jobs.[22]

While some white workers supported the civil rights movement of the 1960s, most did not, and the labor movement, including such presumably liberal unions as the United Auto Workers, opposed it until it became politically necessary to give it at least lukewarm approval.[23] Today, nearly thirty years after the passage of the Civil Rights Act, unions still find themselves litigants in racial suits, and racism is still virulent within the unions and within the working class as a whole.

We need now to look at the current state of the labor movement in the United States, but first we need to make it clear why the *labor* movement is so important. There may be many progressive movements—feminist, anti-racist, gay and lesbian liberation, and environmental movements, all of which are pushing for a more egalitarian and humane society. What gives the labor movement its special place, however, is that it is *capitalism,* and not sexism, racism, or homophobia, that has generated the results described in the previous chapters, and it is *capitalism* that must give way to a different system of production and distribution. To fundamentally change any economic system, it is necessary to pay particular attention to *work*—to who controls it, to the way it is done, and to the ways in which the fruits of human labor are to be shared. It is the exploitation of *workers* that is fundamental to capitalism, and it is this exploitation that must come to an end. A labor movement is the natural agent of such radical change.

Having said this, it must also be noted that a labor movement divided by sexism and racism and unconcerned with the destruction of the environment will not be able to take the lead as an agent of change. Therefore, it is essential that the labor movement make common cause with *all* progressive movements, building what Jeremy Brecher and Tim Costello call "labor-community coalitions" that challenge corporate capital.[24] After all, capitalism is more than just an economic system: it is also a culture, insinuating its ethos of selfishness into every sphere of life. This means that this culture must be attacked on all fronts at all times.

THE STATE OF THE U.S. LABOR MOVEMENT

Despite the fact that unions significantly improve workers' benefits and wages and make them less susceptible to corporate power (see Figure 6-3), the U.S. labor movement is a long way from realizing its potential power. This can be seen in any number of statistics. First, union density in the United States (defined as the percent of total civilian wage and salary employees who are union members) is among the lowest of all of the advanced capitalist nations.[25] This is shown in Figure 6-4. Second, union density in the United States has been decreasing since the middle of the 1950s. In 1955 it was approximately 33 percent, the highest in the history of the nation. By 1970 it was 30 percent, and in 1980 it was between 22 and 25 percent (depending on the source of the data). During the 1980s, union membership went into free fall,

Figure 6-3
Union-Nonunion Earnings Gap, 1989

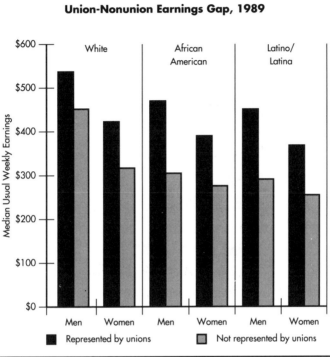

hitting 16 percent by 1990.[26] Some of our largest and strongest unions lost hundreds of thousands of members during the 1980s. For example, membership in the United Steel Workers fell from 964,000 in 1979 to 459,000 in 1991, and the United Auto Workers lost 134,000 members between 1985 and 1991.[27]

Researchers have pointed to various reasons for this decline.[28] For one thing, as capital has shifted out of manufacturing and into services and finance, union density dropped because the former sector was much more heavily unionized than the latter. The same argument can be made for the shift of capital from the highly unionized Northeast and Midwest to the nonunion South

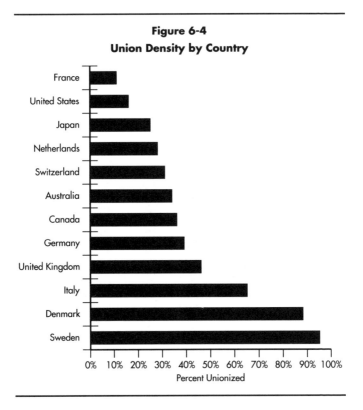

Figure 6-4
Union Density by Country

and West. However, these capital movements do not account for all of the loss. Two other factors are important. First, most unions, once they consolidate their position within a particular industry, drastically curtail their organizing efforts. As a result, the share of union revenues devoted to organizing new members falls and fewer new workers join. Organizing a union is hard work and takes both time and money. Unfortunately, unions like the United Auto Workers have been unwilling to move beyond the large industrial plants that formed the bedrock of their membership, despite changes in the organization of the industry. And inside the auto factories, the union has relied on union security agreements to compel newly hired workers to join the union but has failed to make these workers understand the need for union membership.

The second factor in the decline in union density is the increasingly widespread corporate contempt for labor laws.[29] As stagnation and intense international competition battered the economy, the large corporations scuttled the postwar accord with organized labor. Aided by the government, businesses began to commit unfair labor practices with impunity, firing union sympathizers and refusing to negotiate contracts with legally established unions. Most of the violators of the law went unpunished, and those that were prosecuted suffered penalties so modest that the average business executive concluded that the benefits of breaking the law far outweighed the costs of getting caught.

Another indication of organized labor's weakness is the number of strikes undertaken by the unions. The strike has been the workers' main weapon, and while changes in corporate organization have made this problematic, well-organized strikes can still be a very effective deterrent to corporate power. Figure 6-5 shows the drastic drop in the number of major strikes—those involving at least 1,000 workers and lasting more than one day. The forty work stoppages that took place in 1991 was the lowest number since stoppages were first counted in 1947.

Today, employers are willing to take on any striking union and hire scabs in situations where this would have been unthinkable two decades ago. For a union to win a strike today, it must do a lot more than simply set up picket lines. It must be willing to make alliances with a wide range of potential allies and actively organize entire communities. It must use imaginative tactics, such as corporate campaigns that target the struck corporation's customers and resource and financial suppliers. The sad fact is that not many unions are willing to do these things. In fact, in some cases—notably the strike of Hormel workers in Austin, Minnesota, in 1985-1986—national unions have *punished* local unions that have militantly defended their rights.[30]

Figure 6-5
Number of Strikes per Year, 1969–1991

A final measure of the labor movement's lack of power is its political impotence. The heady days of the 1930s and World War II, when the support of the trade unions was actively courted by politicians, are long gone. From the passage of the Taft-Hartley Act in 1947 until the present day, labor's political decline has been visible to all. Not one anti-labor provision of Taft-Hartley has been repealed (although some were invalidated by the courts). What is worse, many supposedly progressive unions used the anti-communist provision of the act to purge their own progressive leaders and rank-and-file members.[31] In 1977, with a Democratic President and Democratic control of both houses of

Congress, the AFL-CIO was unable to secure passage of mild labor reform.

MR. VOLCKER COMES TO JOHNSTOWN   During the deep recession of 1982-1983 the town in which I was living, Johnstown, Pennsylvania, had the nation's highest rate of unemployment, nearly 30 percent. Employment in the steel mills that had once given the town its prosperity fell from over 10,000 to about 2,000. No one could find a job, and folks were becoming desperate. In the bars that I frequented, the bartender and I would often be the only employed people. In the midst of this crisis, Paul Volcker, chairman of the Board of Governors of the Federal Reserve System, came to town to give a speech at the local country club. Volcker had ruthlessly engineered the depression by pushing interest rates up to record levels. His goal was to eliminate inflation (which, remember, the banks hate) by causing so much unemployment that workers would have to take pay cuts for years to come. It was amazing to see that not one local union protested Volcker's appearance. There were no pickets, no leafletting, no angry letters to the editor. Nothing. Volcker was hailed as some sort of economic savior. If the labor movement had had a coherent program, with a plan for reversing the economic decline, such a lack of response would have been impossible. This was not and is not the case, and the truth is that most rank-and-file steelworkers did not know who Volcker was or what he had done.

WHAT IS TO BE DONE?

In earlier chapters I examined concrete programs that might alleviate the economic misery that engulfs working people. Let me summarize some of these.

First, there is no good financial or economic reason why employment cannot be guaranteed as a matter of public policy. There are innumerable unsatisfied social needs, from child care to housing to health care—not to mention massive construction of roads, railroads, bridges, and public transportation. Guaranteed employment could be tied to a massive economic reconversion away from military spending and toward the production of socially useful and environmentally friendly goods and services. At the same time, the actual production and management of this production could be done at as decentralized a geographic level as possible. Daycare, for example, should be funded (and minimum standards set) by the federal government, but its actual provision and control should be local. As Staughton Lynd points out, the provision of legal services to poor people through the Legal Services Corporation could serve as a model for the provision of a host of social services.[32] The costs associated with a full employment policy can be financed progressively through taxation and bond sales.

Second, the minimum wage must be increased so that full-time workers earn at least enough money to support a family of four at the poverty level of income. Any jobs lost as a result should be absorbed by public employment.

Third, universal and comprehensive health care must be provided to everyone. Democratically managed and federally financed health care organizations should be established, and these can also be an important source of public employment. If health care were provided in this way, it would be possible for many low-wage workers to live adequately, and it would increase the power of all workers by removing a major source of financial worry.

Fourth, there must be a reduction in the average hours of work for those who work full-time.[33] It is not healthy for people to work sixty and seventy hours a week, year in and year out, and it is hardly rational that hours of work should be increasing for some while millions of others cannot find any work at all. This reduction in hours could be achieved if unions made it a priority, pressing hard for increased vacations, leaves, and holidays, and looking toward a four-day week and a six-hour day—as they have been in Europe with some success. If fringe benefits were provided for all contingency workers, the necessity for multiple jobs and the accompanying long hours would be reduced. Workers must be given a chance to work fewer hours in place of wage increases, or to have some of both. Overtime work could be compensated with future time off, and workers could accumulate hours to use for long vacations or leaves. Research indicates that many workers would take shorter hours if given the opportunity. The government must mandate minimum vacations, parental leaves with pay, sabbaticals, and so forth, for all workers, as many other countries already do. And finally, we must abandon the notion that happiness can only be achieved by consuming things.

Fifth, controls must be placed on what the wealthy can and cannot do with their wealth. Abandoned plants can be nationalized, and plans developed so that the property can be leased to the former workers and/or the communities in which the plants are located.[34] Before plants relocate, the owners must assume some financial responsibility for their employees and the towns and cities that have been so generous to them over the years. With respect to the internationalization of capital, trade agreements must be negotiated to establish rules that corporations must abide by no matter where they are located. The government should refuse to give aid or support to any nation that refuses to enforce these rules, and corporations should risk nationalization if they do not obey them. Such rules would include a minimum wage, respect for the rights of workers to organize and bargain collectively, strict environmental standards, restrictions on child labor, and the like. All international financial institutions—including the World Bank and the International Monetary Fund—must also act in accord with strict social standards, giving the best deals not to those countries that repress their people but to those that honor human rights.

Sixth, any and all noncapitalist forms of production must be tried and encouraged. Worker collectives and cooperatives, community- and worker-controlled firms, and employee stock-ownership plans must have access to public funds, accumulated perhaps in public investment banks. Economist Robert Pollin has suggested that the Federal Reserve banks should be converted into public banks.[35] As people start to see that goods and services can be provided without strict adherence to the goal of maximum private profit, they will start to see the possibility of a radically new economic system. Capitalism began within the shell of feudalism, eventually breaking out of this shell and proclaiming its independence. Similarly a new system could grow within capitalism and eventually replace it.

At this point, readers should ask themselves which choice is more realistic: to seek liberating and progressive ways to reduce human misery or to continue along our current path, which is bound to increase this misery geometrically? As bad as things are here, they are worse in most of the rest of the world, and they will get worse here. People are sick of business as usual, and when they have the facts and the organization, they can and will bring about the needed radical change.

NOTES

CHAPTER 1: INTRODUCTION

1. Jerry Kloby, "The Growing Divide: Class Polarization in the 1980s," *Monthly Review* 39, no. 4 (September 1987): 7.
2. Lawrence Mishel and Jared Bernstein, *The State of Working America*, (Armonk, NY: M.E. Sharpe, Inc., 1993), p. 46.
3. Ibid., p. 274.
4. Ibid., pp. 287, 290.

CHAPTER 2: EMPLOYMENT: FALLING WAGES AND INCOMES

1. Mishel and Bernstein, *The State of Working America*, p. 194.
2. Schor, *The Overworked American* (New York: Basic Books, 1991), p. 29.
3. Mishel and Bernstein, *The State of Working America*, p. 132.
4. Schor, *The Overworked American*, p. 29.
5. Ibid., p. 35.
6. Polly Callaghan and Heidi Hartmann, *Contingent Work: A Chart Book on Part-Time and Temporary Employment* (Washington, DC: Economic Policy Institute, 1991), p. 1.

7. Ibid., p. 6.

8. Ibid., p. 8.

9. Ibid.

10. Lawrence Mishel and Ruy A. Teixeira, *The Myth of the Coming Labor Shortage* (Washington, DC: Economic Policy Institute, 1991), p. 11.

11. Ibid., p. 20.

12. Quoted in ibid., p. 24.

13. Mishel and Bernstein, *The State of Working America*, p. 194.

14. Ibid., p. 195.

15. See, for example, Ronald B. Mincy, "Raising the Minimum Wage: Effects on Family Poverty," *Monthly Labor Review* 113, no. 6 (July 1990): 18-25; Linda R. Martin and Demetrios Giannaros, "Would a Higher Minimum Wage Help Poor Families Headed by Women?," *Monthly Labor Review* 113, no. 8 (August 1990): 33-37.

16. This material is taken from an excellent pamphlet by William O'Hare et al., *Real Life Poverty in America* (Washington, DC: Population Reference Bureau, Inc. and Center on Budget and Policy Priorities, 1990).

17. Mishel and Bernstein, *The State of Working America*, p. 276.

18. Ibid., p. 156.

19. Ibid.

20. Ibid., p. 276.

21. Ibid., p. 140.

22. Ibid., p. 142.

23. See Paul Krugman, "The Rich, the Right, and the Facts," *The American Prospect* 11 (Fall 1992): 19-31.

24. See on this and related issues the fine book in this series by Teresa Amott, *Caught in the Crisis: Women and the U.S. Economy Today* (New York: Monthly Review Press, 1993), specifically pp. 77-78.

CHAPTER 3: EMPLOYMENT: INCREASING HOURS AND JUNK JOBS

1. Mishel and Bernstein, *The State of Working America*, pp. 132, 134.

2. Juliet Schor, *The Overworked American* (New York: Basic Books, 1991), p. 29.

3. Ibid., p. 11.

4. The calculations in this paragraph are taken from data in Mishel and Bernstein, *The State of Working America*, pp. 69-83.

5. Schor, *The Overworked American*, p. 30.

6. Ibid., p. 31.

7. Mishel and Bernstein, *The State of Working America*, p. 238.

8. Ibid., p. 241.

9. Ibid., p. 242.

10. Schor, *The Overworked American*, p. 31.

11. Ibid., pp. 67-68.
12. Mishel and Bernstein, *The State of Working America*, p. 174.
13. Callaghan and Hartmann, *Contingent Work*, p. 24.
14. Mishel and Bernstein, *The State of Working America*, p. 188.
15. Ronald G. Ehrenberg and Robert S. Smith, *Modern Labor Economics*, 4th ed. (New York: HarperCollins, 1991), p. 450.
16. Cited in Mishel and Teixeira, *The Myth of the Coming Labor Shortage*, p. 11.
17. Ibid., p. 15.
18. Ibid.
19. Robert Pollin, "Use Conversion to Create Jobs," *The Nation*, 12 July 1993, p. 66.
20. Harry Braverman, *Labor and Monopoly Capital: The Degradation of Work in the Twentieth Century* (New York: Monthly Review Press, 1974).
21. Mishel and Teixeira, *The Myth of the Coming Labor Shortage*, p. 23.
22. An excellent critical work on the new management, with a good case study of NUMMI, is Mike Parker and Jane Slaughter, *Choosing Sides: Unions and the Team Concept* (Boston: South End Press, 1988).
23. The data in the next four paragraphs are taken from Mishel and Bernstein, *The State of Working America*, p. 237, and Callaghan and Hartmann, *Contingent Work*, pp. 9-29.
24. Callaghan and Hartmann, *Contingent Work*, p. 17.
25. Ibid., p. 28.
26. Philip Mattera, *Prosperity Lost* (Reading, MA: Addison-Wesley, 1990), p. 86.
27. Ibid., p. 91.
28. Ibid.
29. Callaghan and Hartmann, *Contingent Work*, p. 8.

CHAPTER 4: UNEMPLOYMENT

1. Philip Harvey, *Securing the Right to Employment* (Princeton, NJ: Princeton University Press, 1989), pp. 3-4, 127.
2. See Frances Fox Piven and Richard Cloward, *Regulating the Poor: The Functions of Public Welfare* (New York: Vintage Books, 1971), pp. 3-42.
3. Still one of the best descriptions of the horrors of work in early capitalism is the chapter titled "The Working Day" in Karl Marx, *Capital*, vol. I (New York: Vintage Books, 1977), pp. 340-416.
4. E.P. Thompson, *The Making of the English Working Class* (New York: Pantheon Books, 1964).
5. For a summary of the methodology used in the household survey, see U.S. Department of Labor, *Handbook of Labor Statistics* (Washington, DC: U.S. Government Printing Office, 1989), pp. 1-6.

6. Council of Economic Advisors, *Economic Report of the President* (Washington, DC: U.S. Government Printing Office, 1985), pp. 232-33.
7. Ibid., pp. 232-33.
8. *Handbook of Labor Statistics*, pp. 138-41, 27-29.
9. These results have been repeated throughout 1993. See the brief summary in Dean Baker, "Job Drain," *The Nation*, 12 July 1993, p. 68.
10. Callaghan and Hartmann, *Contingent Work*, pp. 3-4; Mishel and Bernstein, *The State of Working America*, p. 216.
11. Paul Baran and Paul Sweezy, *Monopoly Capital* (New York: Monthly Review Press), 1969, pp. 237-42.
12. M. Harvey Brenner, "Economy, Society and Health," paper prepared for the Conference on Society and Health, Harvard School of Public Health, 16 October 1992.
13. See William P. O'Hare et al., *African Americans in the 1990s* (Washington DC: Population Reference Bureau, Inc., 1991); Elizabeth C. Kim, "Toward a Cord of Solidarity: Progressive Social Change in the 1990s," *Monthly Review* 45, no. 4 (September 1993): 55.
14. U.S. Department of Commerce, *Statistical Abstract of the United States* (Washington, DC: U.S. Government Printing Office, 1992), pp. 120, 197.
15. *Handbook of Labor Statistics*, pp. 138-41.
16. Harvey, *Securing the Right to Employment*, pp. 51-53.
17. Mishel and Bernstein, *The State of Working America*, p. 302.
18. Ibid., p. 304.
19. Richard A. Cloward and Frances Fox Piven, "The Fraud of Workfare," *The Nation*, 24 May 1993, pp. 693-96.
20. Robert Scheer, "Trouble Still in Forrest City," *The Nation*, 22 March 1993, pp. 370-74.
21. Nancy Rose, *Put to Work: Relief Programs of the Great Depression* (New York: Monthly Review Press, 1994), pp. 104-5.
22. Franklin Folsom, *Impatient Armies of the Unemployed* (Niwot, CO: University Press of Colorado, 1991), pp. 231-431.
23. Isaac Shapiro and Marion Nichols, *Far from Fixed* (Washington, DC: Center on Budget and Policy Priorities, 1992.
24. Quoted in Folsom, *Impatient Armies of the Unemployed*, p. 217.
25. Harvey, *Securing the Right to Employment*, pp. 21-50.
26. See Jeremy Brecher, "Global Unemployment at 700 Million," *Z Magazine* 6, no. 11 (November 1993): 45-48.

CHAPTER 5: THE NATURE OF THE BEAST

1. For a good description of economic systems and what economics is, as well as a strong critique of mainstream economics, see Paul M. Sweezy, *The*

Theory of Capitalist Development (New York: Monthly Review Press, 1956), pp. 3-8.

2. Karl Marx, *Capital*, vol. 1, pp. 247-57.
3. There are many books that examine the conflict between capital and labor. One of my favorites is Jeremy Brecher, *Strike!* (San Francisco: Straight Arrow Books, 1973).
4. See Braverman, *Labor and Monopoly Capital*; Parker and Slaughter, *Choosing Sides*; and Dan Clawson, *Bureaucracy and the Labor Process* (New York: Monthly Review Press, 1980).
5. For a chilling account of early factories in the context of the great rebellion of weavers against the owners of the machines that were ruining their lives, see the novel by Glyn Hughes, *The Rape of the Rose* (New York: Simon and Schuster, 1993).
6. A popular account of this perspective is Milton Friedman and Rose Friedman, *Free to Choose: A Personal Statement* (New York: Harcourt Brace Jovanovich, 1980).
7. E. K. Hunt and Howard Sherman, *Economics: An Introduction to Traditional and Radical Views*, 5th ed. (New York: Harper and Row, 1986), Chaps. 7 and 32.
8. What follows is a simplified version of the theory laid out by the "Monthly Review" school, first put forward by Baran and Sweezy in *Monopoly Capital* and since explicated in books and essays by the editors of *Monthly Review*.
9. John M. Keynes, *The General Theory of Employment, Interest, and Money* (London: Macmillan, 1936).
10. Paul M. Sweezy, "What's Wrong with the American Economy," *Monthly Review* 36, no. 1 (May 1984): 7.
11. This was the word used by Keynes' more radical followers, such as Joan Robinson.
12. Harry Magdoff, "International Economic Distress and the Third World," *Monthly Review* 33, no. 11 (April 1982): 3-5.
13. See Arthur MacEwan, "World Capitalism and the Current Economic Crisis," in Richard C. Edwards, Michael Reich, and Thomas E. Weisskopf, eds., *The Capitalist System*, 3rd ed. (Englewood Cliffs, NJ: Prentice-Hall, 1986), pp. 390-96.
14. David Milton, *The Politics of U.S. Labor: From the Great Depression to the New Deal* (New York: Monthly Review Press, 1982).
15. See Samuel Bowles, David M. Gordon, and Thomas E. Weiskopf, "The Rise and Demise of the Postwar Corporate System," in Edwards, Reich, and Weiskopf, eds., *The Capitalist System*, pp. 379-90.
16. Ibid., p. 384.
17. Economic Strategy Institute, *An Economic Strategy for America: A Blueprint for American Revitalization* (Washington, DC: Economic Strategy Institute, 1992), p. 27.

18. There are many good books about the Vietnam war. An exceptional account of it, and of U.S. imperialism in general, is Noam Chomsky and Edward S. Herman, *The Political Economy of Human Rights,* 2 vols. (Boston: South End Press, 1979).
19. Kim Moody, *An Injury to All* (London and New York: Verso, 1988), pp. 95-146.
20. Ibid., p. 102.
21. Cited in John Borsos, "General Motors Versus the People of Ypsilanti, Michigan," *Z Magazine* 6, nos. 7/8 (July/August 1993): 26.
22. See Michael D. Yates, *Labor Law Handbook* (Boston: South End Press, 1987).

CHAPTER 6: WHAT IS TO BE DONE?

1. Robert Sherill, "S&Ls, Big Banks and Other Triumphs of Capitalism," *The Nation,* 19 November 1990, pp. 588-623.
2. Mishel and Bernstein, *The State of Working America,* p. 387.
3. Ibid.
4. Ibid., p. 400.
5. Andrew L. Shapiro, *We're Number One* (New York: Vintage Books, 1992), p. 8.
6. Ibid., p. 17.
7. See Vicente Navarro, "Swaying the Health Care Task Force," *The Nation,* 6/13 September 1993, p. 229.
8. Michael Albert, "Society's Pliers: Deficit and Debt," *Z Magazine* 6, no. 3 (March 1993): 11-14; see also Alexander Cockburn, "Beat the Devil," *The Nation,* 12 October 1992, p. 387.
9. Albert, "Society's Pliers," p. 12.
10. Mishel and Bernstein, *The State of Working America,* p. 408.
11. Harvey, Securing the Right to Employment, pp. 43-50.
12. C. Wright Mills, *The Power Elite* (New York: Oxford University Press, 1965); G. William Domhoff, *The Higher Circles: The Governing Classes in America* (New York: Random House, 1970).
13. Moody, *An Injury to All,* p. 128.
14. Ibid.
15. Yates, *Labor Law Handbook,* pp. 150-53.
16. See the chapter on Sweden in Andrew Zimbalist et al., *Comparing Economic Systems* (New York: Harcourt Brace Jovanovich, 1989).
17. See "Turning Up the Heat," *United Mine Workers Journal* 104, no. 5 (June 1993): 4-7; and Michael D. Yates, "From the Coal Wars to the Pittston Strike," *Monthly Review* 32, no. 2 (June 1980): 36-37.
18. The Editors, "The Uses and Abuses of Measuring Productivity," *Monthly Review* 32, no. 2 (June 1980): 1-9.

19. Schor, *The Overworked American*, p. 2.
20. See the special issue of the journal *Labor History* 34, nos. 2-3 (Spring-Summer 1993) for some interesting discussions of the intersections of gender and class.
21. David Roediger, *The Wages of Whiteness: Race and the Making of the American Working Class* (London: Verso, 1991); see also Philip Foner, *Organized Labor and the Black Worker, 1619-1973* (New York: Praeger, 1974).
22. See Herbert Hill, "Black Workers, Organized Labor, and Title VII of the 1964 Civil Rights Act: Legislative History and Litigation Record," in Herbert Hill and James E. Jones, Jr., eds., *Race in America: The Struggle for Equality* (Madison: University of Wisconsin Press, 1993), pp. 263-344.
23. Ibid.
24. Jeremy Brecher and Tim Costello, eds., *Building Bridges: The Emerging Grassroots Coalition of Labor and Community* (New York: Monthly Review Press, 1990).
25. Clara Chang and Constance Sorrentino, "Union Membership Statistics in 12 Countries," *Monthly Labor Review* 114, no. 12 (December 1991): 48.
26. Ibid.
27. U.S. Department of Commerce, *Statistical Abstract of the United States, 1992*, p. 421.
28. See Richard Freeman and James Medoff, *What Do Unions Do?* (New York: Basic Books, 1981); Michael Goldfield, *The Decline of Organized Labor in the United States* (Chicago: University of Chicago Press, 1987).
29. Paul Weiler, "Promises to Keep: Securing Workers' Rights to Self-Organization Under the NLRA," *Harvard Law Review* 96, no. 8 (June 1983): 1769-1825.
30. Peter Rachleff, *Hard-Pressed in the Heartland: The Hormel Strike and the Future of the Labor Movement* (Boston: South End Press, 1993).
31. See the relevant essays in Ann Fagan Ginger and David Christiano, eds., *The Cold War Against Labor*, 2 vols. (Berkeley: Meiklejohn Civil Liberties Institute, 1987). See also William E. Forbath, "The Shaping of the American Labor Movement," *Harvard Law Review* 102, no. 6 (April 1989): 1111-1256.
32. Staughton Lynd, "From Protest to Economic Democracy: Labor-Community Ownership and Management of the Economy," in Brecher and Costello, eds., *Building Bridges*, pp. 259-73. See also Michael Albert and Robin Hahnel, *The Political Economy of Participatory Economics* (Princeton, NJ: Princeton University Press, 1991).
33. This paragraph relies upon Schor, *The Overworked American*, pp. 139-66.
34. Lynd, "From Protest to Economic Democracy," pp. 272-73.
35. Robert Pollin, "Transforming the Federal Reserve into a Public Investment Bank," unpublished paper, 1992.

SOURCES FOR FIGURES AND TABLES

Figure 2-1: Data from Mishel and Bernstein, *The State of Working America*, Table 3.39.

Figure 2-2: Ibid., Table 3.23.

Figure 2-3: Figure from Amott, *Caught in the Crisis*, p. 47.

Figure 3-1: Data from Mishel and Bernstein, *The State of Working America*, Table 1.2.

Figure 3-2: U.S. Bureau of Labor Statistics, *Handbook of Labor Statistics, 1989*, Tables 5 and 55; U.S. Bureau of Labor Statistics, *Employment and Earnings*, various issues; Council of Economic Advisors, *Economic Report of the President 1993*, Table B-34.

Figure 3-3: Data from Mishel and Bernstein, *The State of Working America*, Table 1.24.

Figure 3-4: Ibid., Table 3.25.

Table 4-1: Harvey, "Economy, Society and Health," p. 6.

Figure 4-1: Richard DuBoff, "Unemployment in the United States," *Monthly Review* 29, no. 6 (October 1977): 11; U.S. Bureau of Labor Statistics, *Monthly Labor Review,* various issues. The sampling procedure described in the text has been used since 1940. The rates in the figure for the years before 1940 represent the best estimates that statisticians have been able to make with the data available. The rates for 1890 through 1939, therefore, are probably less reliable than those since 1940.

Figure 4-2: Data from Mishel and Bernstein, *The State of Working America*, Table 3.39.

Figure 4-3: U.S. Bureau of Labor Statistics, *Handbook of Labor Statistics, 1989*, Table 29; U.S. Bureau of Labor Statistics, *Employment Situation,* various issues, Table A-7.

Figure 4-4: Figure from Amott, *Caught in the Crisis*, p. 62.

Figure 5-1: Council of Economic Advisors, *Economic Report of the President 1986*, Table B-2.

Figure 5-2: Samuel Bowles et al., "An Economic Strategy for Progressives," *The Nation,* 10 February 1992, p. 163.

Figure 5-3: Figure from Amott, *Caught in the Crisis*, p. 120.

Figure 6-1: Figure from Vicente Navarro, *Dangerous to Your Health* (New York: Monthly Review Press, 1993), p. 16.

Figure 6-2: Ibid., p. 67.

Figure 6-3: Figure from Amott, *Caught in the Crisis*, p. 66.

Figure 6-4: Chang and Sorrentino, "Union Membership Statistics in 12 Countries," p. 48. The figures for Italy and the U.K. are for 1988 and the figures for Sweden, Germany, and France are for 1989; all the other figures are for 1990.

Figure 6-5: U.S. Department of Commerce, *Statistical Abstract of the United States, 1992*, p. 421.

INDEX